Concept Cars

MACHINES THAT PUSH THE BOUNDARIES OF DESIGN

Concept Cars

MACHINES THAT PUSH THE BOUNDARIES OF DESIGN

Richard Dredge

METRO BOOKS
New York

METRO BOOKS
New York

An Imprint of Sterling Publishing
387 Park Avenue South
New York, NY 10016

METRO BOOKS and the distinctive Metro Books logo are trademarks of
Sterling Publishing Co., Inc.

© 2012 by Quantum Publishing Ltd

This 2012 edition published by Metro Books by arrangement with Quantum Books.

All rights reserved. No part of this publication may be reproduced, stored in
a retrieval system, or transmitted, in any form or by any means, electronic,
mechanical, photocopying, recording, or otherwise, without prior written permission
from the publisher.

Publisher: Sarah Bloxham
Managing Editor: Jennifer Eiss
Project Editor: Samantha Warrington
Assistant Editor: Jo Morley
Production: Rohana Yusof
Design: Tim Scrivens

ISBN 978-1-4351-3890-2

For information about custom editions, special sales, and premium and corporate
purchases, please contact Sterling Special Sales at 800-805-5489 or
specialsales@sterlingpublishing.com.

QUCONC

Manufactured in China

2 4 6 8 10 9 7 5 3 1

www.sterlingpublishing.com

Contents

Introduction

Mankind has always wanted to look into the future—and, where possible, to create it, too. After all, isn't it so much more exciting to go somewhere that nobody has ever been? Or do something no one else has ever done? It's only by pushing the boundaries that advances can be made with new designs, new technologies, and new materials. Whether it's clothes, household appliances, or cars, there are always advances to be made, and fashions constantly change, too. Ultimately, concept cars are merely another branch of fashion—one year it's huge wheels while the next it's suicide rear doors. However, there's one thing that doesn't change: the importance of the concept car.

Few concepts ever make it into production, although elements of all of them eventually reach the showrooms. So the concept car is the perfect way of stirring the marketing departments into a frenzy in an attempt to oversell the vehicle. The marketing folks can promise virtually anything—everybody knows they won't have to deliver because it's just an ideas car. Nobody will ever be able to buy it in the form shown. So what's the point? Again, like any branch of the fashion world, it's all about pushing the boundaries. It's not until you've gone too far that you know just how far you can go, and while many concepts aren't really all that adventurous, there are some that are pretty challenging to say the least.

Paul Horrell summed it up very well in writing for *Car* magazine, where he declared that there are five reasons for concept cars, the first being to promote an Italian design house. While concept cars are not exclusively Italian born, Italian designs do account for more than most. The next reason is to soften the public for an impending production car; the third is just to create a distraction while churning out dull cars that do nothing for the company's image. Rejected design proposals and major shifts in a company's design direction are the final two reasons for a company producing a concept car—think about this and you'd be hard pressed to come up with a concept that doesn't fit into one of these categories, and in some cases, more than one.

Above: One of the most outrageous concepts of modern times is Citroën's GT, which started out as a car in a computer game. However, it was too sensational not to make a full-size concept.

Opposite left: General Motors produced three Firebird concepts; this was the first. Harley Earl, the man behind the design, is pictured with his creation. The Firebirds were some of the most farsighted concepts ever made.

Opposite right: Pininfarina's Ferrari-based 512 S Modulo was another concept that was changing the game, but which would never see the light of day in production form. It was unveiled in 1970.

United States

The Buick Y-Job of 1938 is generally acknowledged to be the first true concept car. Designed by Harley Earl of General Motors, this car owed nothing to what had gone before—it was smooth, sleek, aerodynamic, and impossibly stylish. It also remained a one-off because it was simply too daring for prewar car buyers. Although the Y-Job has been credited with launching the whole concept of concepts, there was a car that beat it by five years: the Venus Bilo. I would contend that this was the first true concept car—and even if it can't claim to be that, it most certainly holds greater title to it than Buick's attempt.

Half a decade before Buick's creation was first seen, this test bed from Volvo was shown. The company didn't officially appear as the creator, but Volvo was instrumental in its creation. An independent coach builder created this concept using a Volvo PV653 chassis. When it was unveiled in November 1933 as the Venus Bilo, Volvo claimed to have had no involvement in the projeect; however, it was later disclosed that the car had been built to test reactions to its advanced styling. As well as showing inspiration from contemporary aircraft design, the concept experimented with interior space utilization. Finished in bright blue with beige stripes, the Venus Bilo also examined the idea of removable panels that could easily be replaced in the event of an accident. Once on display, the Venus Bilo drew a very mixed reaction, and although the term "concept car" may not have been around then, that's exactly what the Venus Bilo was.

Despite the Venus Bilo's showing in 1933, it wasn't until the showing of the Y-Job that the floodgates opened for a whole raft of concepts, which were usually referred to as "dream cars." They largely hailed from the United States, with Harley Earl of General Motors being responsible for many of them. He was the man behind the Y-Job, and whereas the Venus Bilo was a one-off that eventually disappeared, Earl's creations were many and varied. The Y-Job survives, and so does the Le Sabre, which arrived in 1951 and was every bit as jaw-dropping as its predecessor. Inspired by jet-fighter aircraft, the Le Sabre made all the contemporary production cars look very dated overnight.

Top: The Venus Bilo was bankrolled by Volvo, but the carmaker didn't admit to it, because the car was considered radical in 1933.

Middle: The Buick Le Sabre, unveiled in 1951, is pictured here with Harley Earl at the wheel.

Bottom: It's Harley Earl with all three of the Firebirds he penned. They were built in 1953, 1956, and 1959 respectively.

Opposite: The world's first official concept car, the Buick Y-Job, arrived in 1938.

As the dream-car phenomenon gained momentum, General Motors cashed in on it by setting up a series of events around the country. Each year the corporation held what it termed a Motorama, where it could show off its latest production models as well as the concepts that were steadily flowing from its design center. The events were full of glitz and glamour, and they ran between 1949 and 1961 in large cities, such as New York, Miami, Chicago, Detroit, Boston, and San Francisco.

It was at these Motoramas that the Firebird series of cars, of which there were four in total, was shown. These were also inspired by jet fighters, each one looking like an aircraft on wheels and each successive version more radical than the last.

With General Motors whipping car buyers into a frenzy, its major rivals had to compete so as not to get left behind, and by 1941, Chrysler was also unveiling dream cars, such as the Thunderbolt. Even the name was exciting—and like the GM cars, the design owed little to anything that was available to buy anywhere. The designer of this concept was Alex Tremulis, who also designed such masterpieces as the Tucker Torpedo and Cord 812—cars that made their mark in history because they went their own way. However, it was Virgil Exner who put Chrysler on the concept car map. He'd worked with Harley Earl at General Motors in the 1930s and was later hired by Chrysler to lead its design studios. By 1950, his first concept was on display: the awkward-looking XX-500. Throughout the 1950s he worked with the Italian coach-building company Ghia to produce a series of concepts, some of which were beautiful, while many of them looked especially awkward. They all had one thing in common: they kept pushing that envelope to see just what was acceptable to a car-buying public.

Europe

While America's Big Three (Chrysler, GM, and Ford) were churning out dream cars to wow U.S. car buyers, in Europe the situation wasvery different. It wasn't until well into the 1950s that things began to settle down after World War II, and although European motor shows took place immediately after the war, it took a while for the various coach builders to start producing their own concepts. The first important concept to be built in Europe was the Bertone-produced BAT 5, which was the first of a trio of concepts all designed to explore aerodynamics. BAT was short for Berlina Aerodynamica Technica, or streamlined, closed touring car, and all three cars were built on Alfa Romeo mechanicals. After the BAT 5 of 1953 came the BAT 7 of 1954 and the BAT 9 followed in 1955—all three cars still exist and their significance is still enormous.

Throughout the 1950s it was left to the Americans to produce most of the seminal concepts, but in 1960 Pininfarina built the X, which featured four wheels in a diamond formation, sported huge rear fins, and threw away the rule book when it came to vehicle packaging and aerodynamics. This was the car as art—a concept that was largely alien to the European carmakers and coach builders until this time. By the mid-1960s, however, Bertone, Pininfarina, and Ghia were all building concepts bearing their own badges and usually— but not exclusively—based on European mechanicals.

By the second half of the 1960s, the Italian concepts were coming thick and fast, but few were being built in other European countries. Cars such as the Marzal (a Bertone design that wore Lamborghini badges), the Bertone Carabo, and the Ferrari 512S (a Pininfarina design) were very significant concepts that were all unveiled in the late 1960s. They were also all outlandish supercars, and although some concepts being produced were more accessible, they were in the minority. This continued to be the theme throughout much of the 1970s, although there was a major distraction at the start of that decade, which accounted for a large chunk of the prototypes that were shown at European motor shows. This was the advent of the safety car, and it seemed that overnight, everyone was jumping on the bandwagon and producing a concept with huge

Top: The Italian carrozzeria built some very farsighted concepts, including the Bertone Marzal, which became the Lamborghini Espada.

Middle: The Bertone Carabo was just as forward-thinking as the Marzal. Marcello Gandini was responsible for its design; he came up with the scissor-action doors.

Bottom: Pininfarina has enjoyed a long and successful relationship with Peugeot, but this Peugette couldn't claim to be a high spot.

Opposite: Of much more interest is the X. It appeared in 1960.

bumpers, immense crash resistance, and thoroughly padded interiors. These concepts were the carmakers' various attempts at building a car that would look after its occupants no matter what; the problem was that, without exception, they were ugly, awful to drive, expensive to produce, and usually heavier than normal, so more fuel thirsty.

By the mid-1970s, the safety cars were just a bad memory, and cars that were more acceptably styled yet still safer than their predecessors were becoming more common. The 1970s also turned the tables in terms of where the important concepts were being produced. After the hedonism of the 1950s and 1960s, things went very quiet in the United States while the focus turned to Europe. Ford had bought the very important Ghia design studio in 1973, and the cars produced after that were seen as European in origin despite the American ownership. Other European coach builders (almost exclusively Italian) continued

to rebody production cars as well as produce bespoke designs. Such companies included Bertone, Zagato, and Pininfarina, and although many of their creations were brand-building exercises, some of them were touted as production-ready cars in the hope that one of the major carmakers might buy an off-the-shelf creation.

By the end of the 1970s, there had been another noticeable shift in emphasis: small car concepts were becoming more common. Such production cars had been very popular in the 1950s, when the microcar market had taken off. Most concepts until this point had been about luxury and performance, or a reinterpretation of something that was reasonably desirable in production form. As the environmental movement started to gain momentum, this move toward creating concepts that were more environmentally friendly suggested that the carmakers were being forced to display a social conscience.

It was also during the 1970s that new aerodynamic technologies began to be pursued more often. Although wind-cheating shapes had been produced several decades earlier, cars such as the Pininfarina CNR explored the boundaries of how slippery it was possible to make a car while still allowing it to carry people and luggage. Madly Impractical cars with incredibly low drag coefficients had been produced before, but they had tended to be single seaters, where the occupant had to drive while semireclining. Innovations, such as flush glazing, more compact power units and transmissions, and lightweight but strong materials, allowed these one-off concepts to be built, but they were still not suitable for mass production. That would come later.

Madly Impractical concepts continued to be built and shown throughout the 1980s and 1990s, but society had changed since the early days. There was still a huge element of fantasy around the car—after all, it represented freedom on wheels. However, social responsibility was also a key ingredient, and as the environmental and safety movements gathered pace, concepts that were safer and kinder to the environment became increasingly commonplace. Although this movement had started in the 1970s, by the 1980s things were becoming a lot more sophisticated. No longer did economical or environmentally friendly necessarily mean stripped-down or basic. Later on, things would get even better with the advent of new methods of propulsion and lightweight materials, but the 1980s saw its fair share of genuinely desirable cars that could conceivably also be affordable and practical. Citroën built its Eco 2000 in 1984, while in 1981 Mercedes unveiled the Auto 2000. Both of these offered practical solutions to transporting families while also being frugal with dwindling fuel reserves, and they incorporated safety systems that later would be the norm.

Concepts that gave a strong hint of impending production models wasn't something that arrived in the 1980s, but it did become more common. Such vehicles in the 1960s and 1970s were usually the preserve of supercars, which were built by hand in tiny numbers. However, by the early 1980s, there were cars such as the Peugeot VERA and Volvo VCC, which would later be available in the showrooms as the 309 and 700 Series, respectively. Other designs were scheduled for production but never made it—the Italdesign Maya being a classic example of such a car. This was built with a midmounted 3-liter V6 engine, the aim being to put it into the showrooms within a couple of years of its 1984 debut. More of a sports car than a supercar, it had everything needed to carry it off, but Ford got cold feet and dropped the project. If only the company had been just a little more ambitious.

Perhaps the most significant change of emphasis that occurred in the 1980s was the arrival of Japanese concept cars en masse. Although Mazda, Toyota, and Nissan had all produced concepts as far back as the 1960s, they hadn't been seen in the United States or Europe, and the country's motoring industry wasn't perceived as a force to be reckoned with. However, that had all changed by the 1980s, as Japanese car sales took off around the world. The companies became richer and were better able to invest in dream cars that showcased their talents—and they were also being taken more seriously in the first place, so their efforts weren't dismissed out of hand.

In the early 1980s, many of the major Japanese companies began building credible concepts, and in many ways they overtook the American and European builders. The styling (and the names!) often

left a lot to be desired, but the engineering and the technology within these cars changed the game. As Japanese companies developed electronics to the point where complex equipment could be reliably installed in cars, concepts suddenly leaped forward. Now it was possible to fit liquid crystal displays (LCDs) and computer-controlled systems in cars.

In the 1990s, carmakers continued in the same vein, but things had gone beyond the mere guaranteed reliability stage. Now production costs of the technology had tumbled as well, so it was expected that even the most basic production car would have computerized systems. That meant the concepts were becoming increasingly complex, while the materials being used in concept car construction had also progressed enormously. The United States got back into the habit of building more concepts in the 1990s, but many of them weren't especially groundbreaking; it was the Japanese and Europeans who did the most interesting examples.

After nearly 80 years since the introduction of the first concept car, things have certainly advanced. Now we routinely see concepts with new methods of propulsion, new body styles, innovative transmissions, and mind-bending levels of equipment. Long may it continue.

Above left: Mercedes created a trio of concepts in the late 1960s and early 1970s, all wearing the C-111 tag. They each trialed a new type of drivetrain technology, with Wankel and diesel engines being tested along with turbocharger installations.

Above right: Although the Ferrari Testarossa of the 1980s was a pretty dramatic car, it looked tame compared with this reskinned version, unveiled as the Pininfarina Mythos in 1989.

Below: The Mazda RX-01 of 1995 showed great promise as a back-to-basics sports car but, unfortunately, the Japanese outfit didn't put the concept into production.

Acura RD-X (2006)

While the rest of the world gets to buy only Hondas, in the ultratough, supercompetitive marketplace that is North America, the Acura is also offered by the same carmaker. That's because the U.S. market was until recently the world's largest and also one of the hardest to crack, which is why some car manufacturers have felt the need to create subbrands. Toyota did it with Lexus, while Nissan launched Infiniti. While those subbrands have since been introduced more widely, Acura is specifically a U.S.-only phenomenon, created because of Honda's everyman image.

When it comes to building brands, however, it's actions that count rather than words, which is why the concept car can be a very powerful marketing tool. That's exactly what Acura counted on when it introduced its RD-X in a bid to tap into the burgeoning compact SUV market of the early twenty-first century.

Honda's own CR-V was proving popular worldwide, but it was seen as a little ordinary; what was needed was something with a bit more pizzazz, and the RD-X was intended to be just that. Targeted at youthful urban professionals, this compact 4x4 with attitude would be just as at home in the city as out on a mountainside with a couple of bikes strapped to the back. When it came to aspirational transport, the RD-X was exactly what it was all about. Well, that's what Acura hoped, anyway.

The first mainstream compact SUV had been Toyota's Rav4, which had never been seen as a car for the enthusiast. After all, SUVs and enthusiastic driving were at odds with each other, but the RD-X aimed to change that with a car that looked like an SUV, was as practical and usable as an SUV, but that offered a driving experience more in keeping with a sports car. Unusually, this initial RD-X concept, introduced at the 2006 New York auto show, was followed up by an identically named SUV that was more conventional—which was no surprise, because it was softening up buyers for the production RDX, which appeared later in 2006.

Above: The RD-X didn't look right from the front, because it appeared as though it didn't feature any headlights—but it did.

Left to Right: That steeply rising waistline looked seriously radical, but no more so than the rear doors, which seemed more as though they belonged on a van from the 1950s. Still, the interior was just as futuristic as the front of the car.

Technology

When the RD-X surfaced, Honda hadn't really embraced diesel power, and besides, U.S. buyers weren't interested in anything other than gasoline-powered SUVs. But in a bid to reduce fuel consumption, Honda fitted its Integrated Motor Assist (IMA) hybrid system, as already seen in its very low-volume Insight. However, while IMA got off to a slow start in Honda's production cars, Toyota's domination of the hybrid market with its Prius encouraged Honda to up the ante. As a result, IMA became more mainstream, with Honda using it in an all-new Insight along with the CR-Z sports coupé and hybrid versions of its Jazz and Civic.

The 2.4-liter gasoline engine in the front of the car would drive the front wheels under only normal conditions. However, when reduced front-end traction was detected, or when a burst of extra speed was required, the electrical system would cut in to power the rear wheels. Each rear wheel was driven by its own electric motor, which was powered by a battery pack that was recharged using regenerative braking.

The transmission was also up to the minute. It was a clutchless manual system inspired by Honda's Formula One racers. Using a computerized clutch system for maximum smoothness, the transmission offered six closely spaced ratios selected via a paddle shifter on the center console. To top things off, the front and rear had independent suspension to ensure that when tackling even the most demanding terrain, there would be plenty of traction as well as comfort.

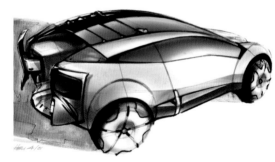

Top: Even concepts can be a letdown after a dramatic sketch has been revealed—but not in the case of the RD-X, which was just as radical in the metal as on the drawing board.

Middle: It was the same for the rear view; indeed, the real thing looked even more dramatic than this early sketch suggested.

Bottom: The RD-X was intended to be practical, which is why there was a usefully sized load bay, which could be accessed via three rear doors.

Opposite: The RD-X's dash succeeded as an ode to minimalism.

Design

Honda, and, hence, Acura, is notoriously conservative with its designs. While it's happy to embrace new technologies head on, out-there styling is not what attracts Acura buyers into showrooms. Despite this, the exterior design of the RD-X was pretty wacky, with its sharply rising waistline along the length of each side door, along with its sculpted wheel arches.

The front of the car featured retractable headlights, although it looked at first glance as though there was no lighting at all. One of the most unusual aspects of the car's styling was its rear, with no fewer than three doors allowing for access to the load bay, the lower two each sliding out of the way. Featuring a lot of glass and brushed alloy, the rear end was effectively an extension of the roof, which was also glass from front to back.

The interior was naturally no less farsighted, with a minimalist look helped by the head-up display for essential information on the move. Instead of door-mounted mirrors, there were rear-facing cameras on each front fender. Each of the two individual rear seats faced slightly outward for extra legroom, while they could also be tipped forward to increase cargo bay space. To enable that space to be used as easily as possible by those with active lifestyles, integral brackets were provided for carrying bikes.

At a Glance

Country of Manufacture
Japan/USA

Engine
Front-mounted, normally aspirated, four-cylinder gas; fuel-injected with integrated motor assist hybrid battery pack

Displacement	2.4 liters
Power	250 bhp
Torque	250 lb.-ft.

Drivetrain
Six-speed clutchless manual transmission, four-wheel drive

Suspension, Wheels, and Brakes
Independent front suspension with disc brakes and 18-in. (249 km/h) alloy wheels

Independent rear suspension with disc brakes and 18-in. (249 km/h) alloy wheels

18-in. (249 km/h) alloy wheels with 235/60 R18 tires all around

Weights and Measurements

Wheelbase	101 in. (2,573 mm)
Length	168 in. (4,265 mm)
Width	75 in. (1,900 mm)
Height	61 in. (1,561 mm)

Performance

Top speed	125 mph (200 km/h) approx.
Debut:	Detroit 2002

Alfa Romeo 8C Competizione (2003)

While some carmakers churn out one concept after another, others are very sparing in their creation of dream cars. Alfa Romeo definitely falls into the latter category, because over the years it's been lucky enough to enjoy a stream of Alfa-badged concepts created by others, such as Italian design agencies Pininfarina and Bertone. These include all-time greats like the Carabo, Canguro, and Nuvola—seminal concepts to which Alfa Romeo lent its name (and often a chassis), but it didn't have to do too much of the donkeywork.

It was a different story here, however, because Alfa produced the 8C itself, with the intention of putting it into limited production. And unsurprisingly, that's exactly what happened; just the briefest of glances confirms that not making even a limited number of this fabulous supercar would have been a travesty. It looked great and drove even better, and with its classic front-mounted V8 and rear-wheel drive, it was a driver's car of the very highest order when it finally did make production.

In the end, Alfa made just 500 examples of the 8C Competizione coupé, and because demand easily outstripped supply, another 500 copies were made—this time of an open-topped edition called the Spider. As such, the 8C was a guaranteed classic straight out of the box, but in many ways the 8C doesn't really sit easily with the rest of the cars in this book, because its styling was very traditional.

Indeed, the 8C was unashamedly retro, so on the face of it this was hardly the same kind of cutting-edge concept that you'll see elsewhere throughout these pages. However, it was still a concept in the truest sense; it was created to test potential buyers' reactions. And most crucially, they liked what they saw, so the 8C made it into production, albeit in limited form.

Above: The 8C was one of the most sensuously designed sports car concepts revealed so far in the twenty-first century; it's perfect from every angle.

Left to right: Even better, when Alfa Romeo put the 8C into production, it didn't water down the design. The only change was the adoption of a conventional hood instead of the forward-hinging front of the car.

Technology

The 8C wasn't a car for exploring the outer limits of technology; as already mentioned, in many ways it was a very traditional concept. This was a car that was more about testing styling themes, even if they were largely somewhat retro. More importantly, however, the 8C was about testing the market—to see whether there were enough buyers out there who were prepared to spend a fairly serious wad of cash on a car sporting mere Alfa Romeo badges. Yes, this admittedly was a brand with a certain amount of cachet, but could Alfa really justify charging more than Maserati money?

It was fitting that the Competizione was priced higher than any of Maserati's mainstream offerings because not only did it pack a Maserati V8, but it was also a lot more exclusive. Under that long hood was a supercharged 4.3-liter engine that could develop a muscular 385 brake horsepower; with the wick turned up this could easily peak at 450 brake horsepower, but Maserati didn't want Alfa Romeo stealing its thunder, so the unit was detuned a little.

That power was fed to the rear wheels via a six-speed Selespeed semiautomatic transmission, and with a 192-mile-per-hour (309-kilometer) top speed, the 8C needed some pretty serious stopping power. As a result, it was fitted with carbon-fiber Brembo brakes, taken straight from the Ferrari Enzo. With the Alfa sharing so many of its oily parts with models from Ferrari and Maserati, it was no wonder that demand outstripped supply.

Top: Incorporating Alfa's classic triangular grille could easily have jarred with all those slippery curves, but it worked perfectly.

Middle: The faired-in headlights were evocative of Alfa's Spider from the 1960s, but behind the glass covers was cutting-edge lighting technology.

Bottom: The ten-spoke alloy wheels were of a three-piece construction. They mixed design simplicity with a high-tech look.

Opposite: The 8C's aerodynamic shape incorporated key styling details to enhance its visual appeal.

Performance

Although the detailing of the 8C Competizione concept was up to the minute, the overall design was more redolent of the great grand tourers of the 1960s, with its faired-in headlights, swoopy curves, and a long hood that hinted at the large-displacement engine that lay beneath. Minimal overhangs front and rear were also intended to give the impression of a muscular V8 in the front of the car, with the power going to the rear wheels.

Crucially, however, the 8C was compact—an essential feature for the agility it would need to see off rivals. As a result, it was around 6 inches (152 millimeters) shorter than a Porsche 911, although that car offered token rear seats whereas the Alfa was strictly a two seater.

Where the 8C really scored, however, was with its detailing, from its 20-inch (508-millimeter) spoked alloy wheels to the chrome adornments in the front of the car. Those muscular front fenders and even more aggressive haunches also looked great, but the best thing was that when the production car arrived, it remained largely faithful to the original concept. There was one key difference, however; while the concept featured a front of the car that tipped forward to give access to the engine, the production car had a conventional hood, which added an extra shut line or two . . . a small price to pay for such a beautiful machine.

At a Glance

Country of Manufacture
Italy

Engine
Front-mounted, supercharged gas V8

Displacement	259 ci (4,244 cc)
Power	410 bhp
Torque	325 lb.-ft.

Drivetrain
Six-speed semiautomatic transmission, rear-wheel drive

Suspension, Wheels, and Brakes
Front suspension: Independent with double wishbones, coil springs, and shock absorbers

Rear suspension: Independent with double wishbones, coil springs, and shock absorbers

Brakes: Ventilated discs front and rear

Front tires: 245/40 ZR20

Rear tires: 275/30 ZR20

Brakes: Carbon-fiber discs by Brembo

Weights and Measurements

Curb weight	3,307 lb. (1,500 kg)
Wheelbase	102 in. (2,595 mm)
Length	168 in. (4,278 mm)
Width	75 in. (1,900 mm)
Height	49 in. (1,250 mm)

Performance

0–62 mph	4.4 seconds
Top speed	192 mph
Debut:	Frankfurt 2003

Audi e-tron/Spyder (2010)

When Audi launched its Quattro in 1980, it went on to create a revolution and, in turn, spur the launch of a separate brand. Always aware of the power of branding, Audi set out to create a new brand in 2009, known as e-tron. The name was used on a purely electric concept car introduced at the Frankfurt Motor Show; Audi's intention after that was to create a whole family of electrically driven cars (as opposed to hybrids), each badged "e-tron."

That first concept looked much like a slightly shrunken R8 coupé, albeit with the obligatory even more eye-catching wheels, grille, and lights. What followed was another car in the same mold, launched a few months later at the 2010 Detroit Motor Show. Also badged e-tron, this new concept looked more production ready in its overall silhouette (if not in its detailing), while still packing a purely electric drivetrain.

Intriguingly, for Audi's next e-tron installment, it resorted to hybrid power—although that newly minted e-tron brand was originally intended to be reserved for cars powered purely by electricity. However, as a hybrid, this new concept was closer to production reality than anything that went before, simply because, when it arrived in 2010, the market still wasn't really ready for cars without any kind of internal combustion engine—especially expensive cars that offered little in the way of usability.

By taking the hybrid route—and a diesel one at that—Audi solved the range anxiety issue. With up to 128.4 miles per gallon (206.6 kilometers per 3.78 liters) possible from the 3.0 TDi powerplant, and a 50-liter fuel tank, it was theoretically possible to cover more than 620 miles (1,000 kilometers) between refueling stops. Realistically, that was at least 500 miles (805 kilometers) more than a typical electric-only car, which made the e-tron far more viable. And while viability hasn't always been a barrier to concept car production, keeping at least one foot firmly planted in the real world can often be a good thing, even if it isn't as much fun.

Above: All of Audi's classic styling cues were used in the front of the e-tron: the oversize grille and the LED headlighting, plus the heavily sculpted hood and wings.

Left to right: After the drama of the car's front of the car, the e-tron's tail was somewhat more subtle. However, the Spyder wasn't subtle at all, although that barchetta-style body looked great from every angle.

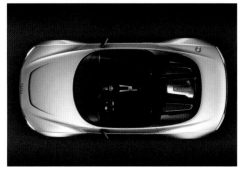

Technology

The big news with the e-tron was its ultrafrugal power train, which emitted just 59 grams per kilometer (two-thirds of a mile) of CO_2 despite a total torque output of 738 lb.-ft. Much of that was due to the twin electric motors, which developed maximum torque at standstill, but Audi's 3-liter diesel V6 engine was also capable of kicking out about 480 lb.-ft. of torque on its own.

By using a diesel/electric drive train, the e-tron featured a 621-mile (1,000-kilometer) range, but even more impressive was the performance offered despite the incredible economy. Not only was the e-tron capable of a rapid 0–62 mph (0–100 km/h) in just 4.4 seconds, but it could achieve a 155 mile-per-hour (250-kilometer) top speed. However, later editions of the e-tron, propelled only by electricity, were restricted to 124 miles (200 kilometers) per hour to conserve the battery.

Although immense fuel efficiency was one of the key requirements of the e-tron's design, so too was driving fun. As a result, there was a short wheelbase for greater agility, while the engine's midmounted position was instrumental in attaining a perfect 50/50 weight distribution. As a result, Audi claimed the concept offered the agility of a go-cart—things helped by the phenomenal torque being distributed between all four wheels, albeit with three-quarters of the torque going to the rear.

The e-tron's agility and efficiency were also aided by its ultralight aluminum body shell. Audi was a pioneer of this method, and through its use, the e-tron's weight was kept down to 3,197 pounds (1,450 kilograms)—pretty good for a car that packed both a diesel engine and an electric drivetrain.

Top: With its mixture of analog and digital instrumentation, the e-tron's cabin effectively mixed old technology with new.

Middle: Audi had been one of the first carmakers to use brushed alloy extensively in its production interiors, so there was aluminum detailing within the e-tron.

Bottom: While the top two pictures show the tan-colored cabin of the 2010 e-tron coupé, Audi opted for a black interior for the Spyder edition that followed later that year.

Design

As with all the best concepts, the first thing that struck onlookers when seeing the e-tron Spyder was its almost complete lack of practicality. At the forefront of this was a lack of weather protection, along with a barchetta-style glasshouse that enclosed the cockpit up to a point, but offered relatively little shielding from the elements.

The sharply tapered front of the car gave a distinctly wedgelike basic shape. The trapeze of the single-frame grille dominated the wedge-shape front of the car and was flanked by two large air intakes, which served as cooling intakes for the electric drive system and also for the TDi engine at the rear of the vehicle.

As had already become Audi's trademark by now, all of the exterior lighting used ultraefficient LED technology. An inventive touch was the charging station for the batteries, which was located beneath Audi's famed four-ring logo. The rings disappeared beneath the front hatch, exposing not just the charging plug but also a display showing the charge state and a map graphic indicating the current electric range.

Another distinctive feature was the set of 20-inch (508-millimeter) wheels, which represented a three-dimensional turbine design. Made of aluminum and carbon, each was made up of an incredible 66 separate components, which meant they were unlikely for production.

Inside, Audi went for the minimalist look—made much easier by the lack of a need for a transmission tunnel or gear selector. With a cockpit oriented toward the driver instead of a conventional instrument cluster, there was simply Audi's trademark MMI (multimedia interface) system flanked by two round dials. The MMI could be controlled via a touch-sensitive panel on the steering wheel, which was flattened off top and bottom in a clear motorsport reference.

At a Glance

Country of Manufacture
Germany

Engine
Midmounted, twin-turbo six-cylinder diesel

Displacement	181 ci (2,967 cc)
Power	296 bhp plus two motors at 86 bhp each
Torque	738 lb.-ft. combined

Drivetrain
Seven-speed, dual-clutch transmission, four-wheel drive, with the engine driving the rear wheels and the electric motors transmitting drive to the front

Suspension, Wheels, and Brakes
Front: Double wishbones and coil springs

Rear: Trapezoidal link

20-in. (508 mm) alloy wheels all around, with 243/30 front tires and 265/30 rear tires

Weights and Measurements

Curb weight	3197 lb. (1,450 kg)
Wheelbase	96 in. (2,430 mm)
Length	160 in. (4,060 mm)
Width	72 in. (1,810 mm)
Height	44 in. (1,110 mm)

Performance

0–62 mph	4.4 seconds
Top speed	155 mph (249 km/h)
Fuel consumption	128.4 mpg
CO_2 emissions	59 g/km
Electric-only range	31 miles (50 km)
Debut:	Detroit 2010

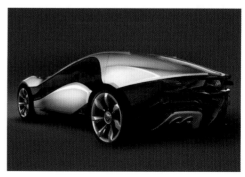

Bertone Pandion (2010)

When the concept car first appeared in the 1930s, it was an expression of what was possible, even if it didn't necessarily reflect where car design was going in the real world. Right up until the 1990s, most concepts were a bit wacky and weren't rooted too much in the real world. Then things started to get watered down, and all too often we started to see previews of production models badged as concepts.

However, in those days of watered-down concept car design, it was Bertone that continued to offer proper dream cars—design studies that didn't really have much hope of ever seeing production. Concepts, such as the BAT5, 7, and 9, and the Carabo, Tundra, and Trapeze were never going to get into a showroom without being vastly watered down—but that didn't stop this Italian design house from pushing the boundaries. And while not all of its concepts have been from another planet, by the first decade of the twenty-first century, Bertone was still steadfastly refusing to dilute things, and the Pandion was the proof.

Yet it nearly didn't happen. Bertone, founded in 1912, filed for bankruptcy protection in 2007 after years of large losses. The operation was saved in 2008, and two years later—Alfa Romeo's centenary year no less—the Pandion was unveiled as proof that the consultancy was well and truly back in business.

The Pandion moniker was chosen because it comes from *Pandion haliaetus*—the scientific name for an Osprey, from which designer Mike Robinson and his team drew inspiration to create the incredible doors that were the standout feature.

Above: Bertone produced some of the seminal concepts in the 1960s and 1970s, but then lost its steam; the Pandion marked a return to form.

Left to right: Apart from those incredible proportions, the most striking thing about the Pandion was that windowline, with its boomerang-shape profile. Because it was based on Alfa Romeo mechanicals, the front of the car also incorporated that marque's triangular grille.

Technology

While the mainstream carmakers were busy churning out concepts that packed the latest fuel-saving technologies, Bertone stuck with good old gasoline and cubic inches—and plenty of them. Underneath that long, low hood was the same 4.7-liter V8 you'd normally find in the front of the car of an Alfa Romeo 8C Competizione. Indeed, the 8C's mechanicals were used pretty much wholesale to underpin the Pandion, which meant the exclusive supercar's brakes, steering, and suspension were all used, along with the engine and transmission.

With such muscle, and a relatively low curb weight of just under 2,870 pounds (1,300 kilograms), the Pandion was a seriously rapid performer. Capable of getting from a standing start to 62 miles (100 kilometers) per hour in just under four seconds, there was also a 199-mile-per-hour (320-kilometer) top speed available—it's a shame Bertone didn't boost the engine's power output a little, just so it could reach that magic double ton. Still, it was unlikely to ever do more than 30 miles (48 kilometers) per hour anyway, so the figure was somewhat meaningless . . .

With so many design details to surprise and delight, Bertone didn't feel the need to overdose on the technology. Indeed, the Pandion was refreshingly simple for a twenty-first-century far-out concept, although there were four LCD screens scattered about the cabin. Three of these were wired up to external cameras to monitor the space around the car; there were no exterior mirrors, because they would have disrupted the flow of the car. The final screen—9 inches (229 millimeters) wide no less—was used to control the Pandion's major functions, such as the climate control, satellite navigation, and entertainment.

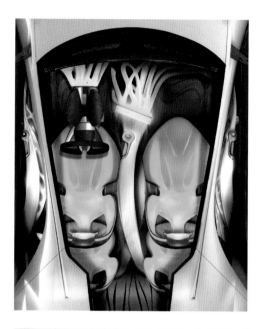

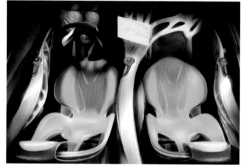

Top: If the exterior of the Pandion looked somewhat wild, it was nothing compared with the cabin, which was equally crazy.

Middle: The cabin was filled with bright blue and white trim materials and was intended to be reminiscent of living organisms—which it was.

Bottom: Believe it or not, there are supposed to be two pairs of seats in there, but those in the back are definitely only for show.

Design

When it comes to unintelligible technobabble, designers are the masters, and nowhere is this more evident than with the Pandion. According to Bertone, the concept's "taut and muscular body" was an original interpretation of the famous Alfa Romeo badge, which features a man-eating serpent and a red cross or "the skin and the frame," as Bertone interpreted it.

However, while the basic silhouette of the Pandion—and even the language used to describe it—was reasonably comprehensible, when it came to some of the detailing, things were anything but clear. Especially where the rear of the car was concerned; here, Bertone reckoned there was a "disembodied or pixelated look," which was meant to represent the tail of a comet. It was this design that was intended to give the Pandion a more dynamic look, so it looked as though it was whizzing along at breakneck speed when it was, in fact, stationary.

Meanwhile, the front of the car featured a long, sculpted sloping hood that was supposed to create the look of a mask, along the lines of the helmets worn by ancient warriors. Again, probably not the first thing that springs to mind, but what couldn't be denied was the Pandion's superb profile, which was sensational, thanks to its cab-rearward stance, helped by those impossibly long doors. Hinged virtually around the axis of the rear wheel, the doors opened by rotating backward, ending up a perfect 90 degrees above the center of the rear wheel. In the process, they lifted up the entire body side of the vehicle, from the front fender to the rear, and when fully open, they were more than 11 feet 10 inches (3.6 meters) high—perfect for those multistory parking ramps.

While the exterior design was one of sensory overload, the interior was somewhat more understated, if no less eye-catching. Bertone claimed it "struck the perfect balance between architectural rigor and the spectacular shapes of living organisms," and for once it was easy to see what the carmaker meant. Alongside the hard, alloy extrusions were flowing shapes for the seats and dash—simple, but spectacular.

At a Glance

Country of Manufacture
Italy

Engine
Front-mounted, normally aspirated gas V8

Displacement	286 ci (4,691 cc)
Power	444 bhp
Torque	350 lb.-ft.

Drivetrain
Six-speed semiautomatic transmission with five driving modes, rear-wheel drive

Suspension, Wheels, and Brakes
Front: Double wishbones with coil springs

Rear: Double wishbones with coil springs

Weights and Measurements

Wheelbase	112 in. (2,850 mm)
Length	182 in. (4,620 mm)
Width	78 in. (1,971 mm)
Height	48 in. (1,230 mm)

Performance

0–62 mph	3.9 seconds
Top speed	199 mph approx.
Debut:	Geneva 2010
Design director:	Mike Robinson

BMW H2R (2004)

When BMW unveiled its H2R concept in 2004, there was great debate about how propulsion technologies would develop for personal transport. Carmakers were developing fuel cells, hybrids, and electric drive while also continuing to advance conventional gasoline and diesel internal combustion engines as far as possible. While BMW had made great strides in creating efficient, refined, and powerful gasoline and diesel engines, it realized that an alternative had to be found; it chose to take the hydrogen route.

BMW had already experimented with hydrogen-powered versions of its existing models, such as numerous 7-Series sedans, by the time the H2R surfaced. While the use of a 7-Series sedan showed that hydrogen technology could be used in a conventional family car—albeit a somewhat generously proportioned one—the H2R wrapped everything up in a skin that was far more eye-catching. However, the basis of both cars was fundamentally the same: the 6-liter V12 gasoline engine that offered power, torque, and uncanny refinement.

Indeed, the H2R used a lot of pretty familiar BMW parts underneath, including components for the brakes, suspension, and steering. Without taking this route, BMW may never have built the H2R at all, because from beginning to end, the whole project took all of ten months to develop, thanks largely to the widespread use of computer-aided design and manufacture.

And while many concepts don't even run, the H2R did more than that: it clinched nine world records at the Miramas Proving Grounds in France in September 2004, including the fastest flying kilometer and mile, along with the quickest standing-start mile and kilometer.

Incidentally, if you're wondering what H2R was short for, BMW offered several answers, so it clearly couldn't make up its mind. On the one hand, H2R was suggested to stand for H Two Race Car, or alternatively it could have been Hydrogen Record Car or even Hydrogen Research Car. And if BMW never worked it out, it's pretty unlikely that anybody else will.

Above: It would be hard to argue that the H2R was a looker from any angle, but this was a superbly efficient shape aerodynamically.

Left to right: The H2R was built with one purpose in mind: to break as many records as possible. As a result, it featured just one seat; this was never meant to be a car with much in the way of practicality.

Technology

At the heart of the H2R was a V12 gasoline engine, but BMW didn't just switch fuels; the power plant was reengineered specifically to run on hydrogen. However, although the H2R was built to run on hydrogen, the V12 could still be fueled by gasoline, if necessary.

The key difference between the gasoline and hydrogen versions of the V12 was the hydrogen injection valve and the choice of materials for the combustion chambers. In the production engine, fuel was injected directly into the cylinders themselves, while the injection valves in the hydrogen engine were integral with the intake manifolds. When the speed records were being attempted, the engine was designed and built for single-mode operation, running exclusively on hydrogen. The key adjustment here was a set of specially made valve seats, because hydrogen doesn't have the lubricating effect of gas. Also, because gaseous hydrogen takes up a larger volume per unit of energy than gas, the hydrogen injection valves had to be larger than conventional injection valve units.

Naturally, safety was of paramount importance with the H2R, which is why its fuel system was state of the art. The vacuum-insulated, double-walled tank, next to the driver's seat, featured no fewer than three valves for optimum safety, while there were also two additional safety valves to deal with leaks in the jacket around the tank. This double safety system guaranteed optimum safety, ensuring the hydrogen tank couldn't burst as a result of excess pressure.

Top: No BMW would be complete without that instantly recognizable double-kidney grille, which is why the H2R's front of the car was dominated by one.

Middle: That droopy front of the car gave the H2R something of a beached-whale look, but those lines were incredibly slippery; the car featured a drag coefficient of just 0.21.

Bottom: For maximum efficiency, the slippery body shell had to be made of lightweight materials, which is why carbon fiber was used throughout.

Opposite: The H2R was undeniably awkward-looking but made up for it with record-breaking speed.

Design

You couldn't really call the H2R a thing of beauty, but as it was created to show what was possible with alternative fuels, you could forgive it at least some of its ugliness. After all, it was capable of great speeds and was amazingly efficient. To that end the H2R was incredibly light and very aerodynamic—it tipped the scales, with fuel and driver, at just 3,439 pounds (1,560 kilograms), while also recording a drag coefficient of just 0.21—most slippery production cars of the time would still have logged a figure of around 0.30.

Because aerodynamic efficiency was the most important thing here, there were no extraneous details for show; everything had to earn its keep. The basic proportions of the H2R were impressive; at 18 feet (5.4 meters) long, its length was comparable with long-wheelbase limousines—yet this was merely a single seater! It was also 7 feet (2 meters) wide, so its footprint was again comparable with luxury cars capable of seating five in comfort.

That ultraslippery body shell was constructed from hyperlight carbon fiber to keep its weight down, and it incorporated numerous aerodynamic features to help reduce drag while also increasing downforce. The key one of these was a diffuser at the rear, which was no less than 8 inches (203 millimeters) long; its job was to cut swirl as much as possible, which might slow the car down.

At a Glance

Country of Manufacture
Germany

Engine
Front-mounted, normally aspirated hydrogen/gas V12

Displacement	364 ci (5,972 cc)
Power	285 bhp

Drivetrain
Six-speed semiautomatic transmission, rear-wheel drive

Suspension, Wheels, and Brakes
Front: Double wishbones with coil springs, anti-roll bar, and aluminum track control arms

Rear: Multilink with anti-roll bar
245/40x19 tires front and rear

Weights and Measurements

Curb weight	3,439 lb. (1,560 kg)
Length	213 in. (5,400 mm)
Width	79 in. (2,000 mm)
Height	53 in. (1,340 mm)
Drag coefficient	0.21

Performance

0–62 mph	6.0 seconds
Top speed	186 mph (299 km/h)
Debut:	Paris 2004

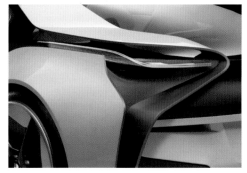

BMW Vision EfficientDynamics (2009)

When BMW creates a concept car, it's either a thinly veiled preview of a forthcoming production model (like the CS1 or xActivity), or it's a full-on test bed for radical ideas that are invariably years away from being a production reality. When it takes the latter route, BMW isn't afraid to push the boundaries—just take a closer look at the Vision EfficientDynamics concept of 2009, which looked like nothing else on the earth and packed some serious farsighted technology beneath that ultradramatic skin.

The premise of the Vision EfficientDynamics was to create a car that was sensational to drive—in terms of performance and handling—while also using as few of the earth's resources as possible. Or as BMW put it, the Vision EfficientDynamics combined the performance of one of the company's M Cars with a level of fuel economy and emissions better than the most recent small production cars. Such a target was only possible by starting from scratch, however, which is why the Vision EfficientDynamics wasn't based on an existing platform and didn't generally use components borrowed from elsewhere within the BMW group.

Such efficiency was also dependent on clever packaging; with batteries, motors, generators, plus a conventional internal combustion engine with transmission to house—along with four occupants and their luggage—the Vision EfficientDynamics was a seriously impressive piece of product design. BMW did it by fitting the engine and its dual-clutch transmission plus one of the motors at the back of the car, with the batteries laid out down its spine, between the left- and right-hand seats. In the front of the car was another electric motor, while the electrics and electronics that controlled everything were also placed between the front wheels—low down to keep the car's frontal area as low as possible.

So why couldn't BMW have just put the Vision EfficientDynamics into production? Unless it had charged a huge amount of money for each one, it just wasn't going to be able to sell the Vision EfficientDynamics profitably.

Above: There was no mistaking which carmaker was behind the Vision EfficientDynamics, thanks to that huge backlit double-kidney grille.

Left to right: Everywhere you looked there were exotic details—even the most mundane items were engineered at a huge expense, including the wheels and lighting. As a result, any production car design would have to be immensely watered down.

Technology

The focus of the Vision EfficientDynamics concept was low fuel consumption above all else. As such, it was fitted with a three-cylinder turbodiesel engine mated to a pair of electric motors—one to drive each axle. This combination provided a peak power output of 356 brake horsepower, along with a ridiculous torque figure of 590 lb.-ft., yet the car was capable of around 75 miles per gallon (31.5 kilometers per liter), despite offering the performance of BMW's hallowed M3. This was because of the light weight and aerodynamics as well as the astonishing efficiency of the power train; running purely on electricity, the emissions of the Vision EfficientDynamics dropped to just 51 grams per kilmometer (about two-thirds of a mile).

On its own, the engine produced 163 brake horsepower, which in itself was impressive; the unit displaced just 1.5 liters, knocking out 109 brake horsepower per liter—phenomenal for a diesel powerplant. The car could run in electric mode for up to 31 miles (50 kilometers), while also using the diesel engine could increase the car's range to more than 430 miles (690 kilometers). The batteries could be topped up by running the diesel engine or through regenerative braking.

The beauty of fitting an internal combustion engine as well as a pair of electric motors was that the Vision EfficientDynamics concept automatically came with four-wheel drive. The result of this was that no matter what the conditions (within reason) the car could put its prodigious power down as effectively as possible, so it was safer as well as more stable and sure-footed.

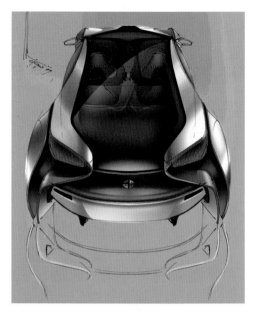

Top: Despite its coupélike profile, there was seating for four. Not that the interior was especially spacious when filled to capacity . . .

Middle: To help with the car's packaging, the seats were ultrathin and made of polycarbonate for strength and lightness.

Bottom: There was a lot of technology packed into the Vision EfficientDynamics; to keep tabs on what it was all doing, there was a multifunction display on the dashboard.

Opposite: This computer simulation demonstrates the Vision EfficientDynamic's "slip."

Design

Thanks to the use of BMW's famous double-kidney grille, from the front it was immediately clear who was responsible for the Vision EfficientDynamics (although from some angles things weren't quite so obvious). The silhouette resembled nothing ever built by BMW before, and the same went for the butterfly doors that swung up to provide access to the four-seater cabin. Those doors—as well as the roof—were equipped with polycarbonate panels that allowed light to flood into the cabin, but if there was a lot of direct sunlight they'd automatically darken to prevent the interior from getting too warm.

While the Vision EfficientDynamic's basic design was pretty amazing, the attention to detail paid to improve aerodynamics and stability were every bit as impressive. With a drag coefficient of just 0.22, the Vision EfficientDynamics was far more slippery than anything in production at the time, by BMW or anyone else. Indeed, such a slippery shape was reckoned to be pretty much on the limit of what's possible, keeping in mind practical issues like fitting in people and motive power, while also offering crash protection.

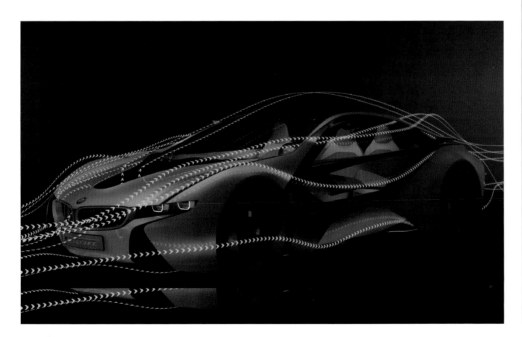

At a Glance

Country of Manufacture
Germany

Engine
Rear-mounted, turbocharged three-cylinder diesel plus 98 lithium polymer battery cells powering electric motors for each axle

Displacement	1.5 liters
Power	356 bhp combined
Torque	590 lb.-ft. combined

Drivetrain
Seven-speed dual-clutch semiautomatic transmission, four-wheel drive

Suspension, Wheels, and Brakes
Unavailable

Weights and Measurements

Curb weight	3,075 lb. (1,395 kg)
Length	181 in. (4,600 mm)
Width	75 in. (1,910 mm)
Height	49 in. (1,240 mm)
Drag coefficient	0.22

Performance

0–62 mph	4.8 seconds
Top speed	155 mph (249 km/h)
Fuel economy	75.1 mpg
CO_2 emissions	99 g/km
Electric-only range	31 miles (50 km)
Debut:	Frankfurt 2009

Cadillac Sixteen (2003)

With Bugatti having unveiled for production a near 1,000-brake horsepower monster, and Maybach having put into production a super-luxury limousine, it was going to take something pretty special from Cadillac to really draw the crowds at the 2003 Detroit Motor Show. And you'd be hard-pressed to argue that the company didn't pull out all the stops with its Sixteen, because this concept combined the most outrageous aspects of both cars—a huge hyper-luxurious bodyshell and a massively powerful engine—in one crazy package.

As company chairman Bob Lutz said: "The Sixteen is a modern interpretation of everything that made Cadillac the standard of the world, and can again. It's a reminder of a glorious past as well as a progressive statement."

It was no coincidence that Rolls-Royce had also unveiled its hyper-luxurious Phantom in 2003, a car with which the Sixteen would have competed directly. In the prewar days of V16 Cadillacs, this American company was seen as the maker of some of the best cars in the world. But its image had slipped in the late-twentieth century, and it was viewed as old-fashioned. However, while Rolls-Royce was in much the same position, its Phantom turned this into a virtue, and the marque successfully played on its traditional qualities. The Sixteen wouldn't play the same card; it would feature high-quality materials throughout, but the technology would be cutting edge.

But all those high numbers relating to power, torque, and cylinders were just an excuse to grab attention. The real reason for the Sixteen was to show people the design direction that Cadillac was aiming to take—a 16-cylinder engine was just a red herring. Sadly, even though the Sixteen was unveiled when the global economy was on a high, the investment required to put the car into production was always going to be massive—and in the certainty that sales of such a car would be absolutely tiny. So as a business case the Sixteen never made sense.

Above: The proportions of the Sixteen were absolutely magnificent, but then an immensely long hood would always be needed to house a 16-cylinder engine.

Left to right: That huge engine—all 13.6 liters of it—generated a lot of heat. As a result, it needed discreet cooling vents in the front fenders to help keep it cool.

Technology

Cadillac introduced the world's first production V16 engine in the 1930s, and with retro being immensely popular when the Sixteen was unveiled, the company reckoned it was only fair to cash in on such a rich heritage. That's why the concept featured a new take on the V16 engine, with a pair of the company's V8s joined together to produce a normally aspirated 13.6-liter powerhouse capable of generating up to 1,000 brake horsepower and an equally ridiculous 1,000 lb.-ft. of torque. All this power was transmitted to the rear wheels via a four-speed automatic transmission.

As a token gesture aimed at keeping the environmentalists happy, the electronics controlling the engine could shut down some of the cylinders so that the fuel consumption, and consequently the emissions, wasn't so frightening. This technology was called "displacement on demand," and it allowed the Sixteen to run on just eight—or even four—cylinders if the power requirements weren't too great. Despite the car's huge dimensions, weight was kept down to a surprisingly low 5,004 pounds (2,270 kilograms), thanks to aluminum being used for much of the car's structure, as well as that enormous engine.

At a time when 20-inch (508 millimeter) wheels were more or less the limit on road cars, as well as concepts, the Sixteen managed to go well beyond this. At each corner of the car there were huge 24-inch (610-millimeter) wheels, housed in rubber band-profile tires—a crazy low-profile 265/40 R24 was used all around.

Top: The driver had an easy time of things, thanks to a very simple dashboard layout. And instead of opting for a glitzy digital display, Cadillac went for analog instruments.

Middle: In-car computers were starting to become a must-have accessory for those who were chauffeured, so the Sixteen featured terminals for computing while on the move.

Bottom: The cabin was filled with exquisite materials, from the finest hides to beautifully presented wood veneers, with plenty of alloy in evidence, too.

Opposite: The Sixteen interior was the height of luxury, with its advanced passenger electronics hidden from view when not in use.

Design

That exterior design was a work of pure genius, because although the Sixteen was more than 18 feet (5.5 meters) long, it didn't look especially big and bulky. The use of a low waistline gave the car more dynamism, and by incorporating subtle aluminum flashes along the flanks, it looked even lower still. The long hood folded in two halves along the centerline of the car, just as Cadillac's prewar cars had done, and in the rear overriders the four exhaust pipes were housed so that they looked completely integrated with the rest of the car.

If the exterior was a work of art, the interior was even more so. The work of Eric Clough, it was a masterpiece of minimalism at first glance. However, everything any occupant could ever need was in there—it just appeared when it was wanted. So although you couldn't see them at first glance, there were computer terminals available, along with a beverage bar and worktables. And yet it was possible to stretch out using the whole length of the interior, because the front passenger seat could be reclined to meet up with the rear seat. This was a car for people who expected to be chauffeured.

At a Glance

Country of Manufacture
USA

Engine
Front-mounted, normally aspirated 90-degree V16 gas; fuel-injected, with displacement on-demand technology, allowing the engine to run on as few as four cylinders when cruising

Displacement	793 ci (13,600 cc)
Power	1,000 bhp
Torque	1,000 lb.-ft.

Drivetrain
Four-speed electronically controlled automatic transmission, rear-wheel drive

Suspension, Wheels, and Brakes
Unequal length double-wishbone suspension at the front, with independent semitrailing arms at the rear

Six-piston calipers fitted front/rear, gripping 16-in. (406-mm) discs at each corner

Weights and Measurements

Curb weight	5,004 lb. (2,270 kg)
Wheelbase	140 in. (3,556 mm)
Length	223 in. (5,673 mm)
Width	69 in. (1,751 mm)
Height	55 in. (1,392 mm)

Performance

0–62 mph	N/A
Top speed	139 mph (224 km/h)

Debut:	Detroit 2003
Exterior designer:	Brian Smith
Interior designer:	Eric Clough

Cadillac Urban Luxury Concept (2010)

Back in the 1950s, when it came to supersize luxury, few could compete with Cadillac. If it was automotive excess you were after, it was Cadillac to which you turned—overblown dimensions, huge engines, massive equipment levels, and unashamed luxury. However, half a century on, the world was a very different place, with fuel shortages and high living costs the order of the day—and that was before an enormous global recession kicked in. Nobody wanted to reduce their standard of living, but everyone needed to downsize—cue the Cadillac Urban Luxury Concept.

The idea of this ultracompact luxury supermini was to offer all the comfort and convenience of a full-size luxury car but without the associated fuel bills or other inflated running costs. A supermini-size Caddy—a sign of the times if ever there was one. However, while the thought of a Cadillac barely bigger than a Smart ForTwo may have seemed incongruous, the company's family look translated rather well onto such a small machine. Although if there was one concept that polarized opinions, this was it.

American buyers couldn't understand why Cadillac would ever build such a tiny car; it made far more sense to sell it with badges from another GM subsidiary, such as Chevrolet. However, the clue was in the name; this was supposed to be a truly luxurious car, despite its diminutive size. And with more and more people worldwide moving to urban areas as cities expanded, it made sense to cater for them by offering transport that combined convenience with comfort.

As with most of the best concepts, this one was never really a serious production proposal. However, with the success of Mini in North America, GM could certainly be forgiven for thinking it was missing a premium small car opportunity. Yet, BMW always had Europe to fall back on if the Mini wasn't a success in the United States; GM wasn't in the same fortunate position with Cadillac.

Above: There's downsizing and there's downsizing; everybody knew the fad had become serious when Cadillac unveiled the tiny Urban Luxury Concept.

Left to right: There had never been a Cadillac as small as this one. For a company used to building leviathans, the Urban Luxury Concept was a major departure—and one that many hoped would never see the light of day as a production car.

Technology

The Urban Luxury Concept was all about economy, so at its heart was a seriously small power plant—the smallest ever fitted to a Cadillac. Displacing just a liter, it was boosted by a turbocharger as well as a hybrid drivetrain, so while no power or torque figures were quoted, they're likely to have been pretty healthy. The hybrid batteries were recharged via the regenerative braking system, so this was very much a car for city life.

For greater ease of use, there was also a dual-clutch semiautomatic transmission that transmitted the power to the front wheels. Cadillac didn't give much away about the car's drivetrain, but it's probable that the electric propulsion would have been directed at the rear wheels to give four-wheel drive when the hybrid system cut in.

With this concept, Cadillac embraced the Internet wholeheartedly in a bid to increase usability and reliability to the max. Just about the whole cabin went digital, so it could be customized or upgraded at the touch of a button, while the detachable control pads could be used for navigation or music. The right-hand touch pad was hidden until deployed or detached by the passenger, who could interact online without compromising the driver's control.

To boost safety, the driver didn't even have to look at the digital displays in front of the steering wheel; instead, he could simply refocus his eyes at the base of the windshield, where there was a head-up display. Also woven into the functionality was GM's OnStar system, with advanced voice recognition interaction, which allowed the driver to do more without compromising safety.

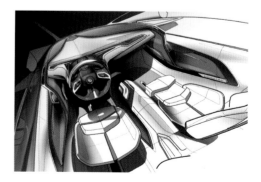

Top: It was a small car, but that was no reason to deny buyers the opportunity to luxuriate in the finest materials.

Middle: To give a greater sense of space, a glass roof was fitted, bathing the car's interior with natural light.

Bottom: The Urban Luxury Concept was billed as a four seater, but the chairs in the back were pretty much useless; this was definitely just a two seater.

Opposite: The Urban Luxury Concept's interior lines match its sleek exterior.

Design

The key thing about the Urban Luxury Concept was its diminutive proportions, along with its short overhangs that really pushed the wheels out to the corners. The result was a cabin that was surprisingly spacious, and while there were officially four seats, anyone sitting in the rear wouldn't want to be very large or they'd soon be uncomfortable.

Despite there being two rows of seats, there was just the one pair of doors, and in true concept fashion they were distinctly unconventional. Lamborghini-style beetle-wing items, the doors added glamour to the car, even if there was little in the way of practicality.

In keeping with the upmarket theme, the cabin featured a lot of high-tech systems for greater space efficiency, while premium materials, such as leather, wood, brushed aluminum, and ceramics, were in abundance. Perhaps best of all, however, was the airiness of the interior; the fixture of glass panels in the roof ensured that if there was any sunshine, it found its way into the Urban Luxury Concept's cabin.

A decent amount of versatilty was also on the menu, although Cadillac made great play of the fact that the front passenger seat was able to slide and recline—just like pretty much any other car on the market then, no matter how cheap or basic. But then sometimes the simplest ideas are also the most useful and user friendly, so why try to reinvent the wheel?

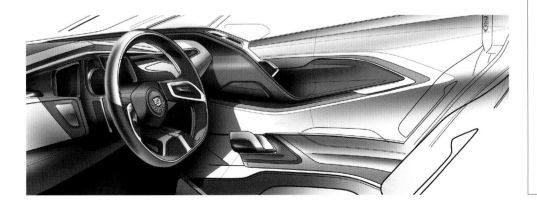

At a Glance

Country of Manufacture
North America

Engine
Front-mounted, turbocharged three-cylinder gas, boosted by a hybrid system

Displacement	1 liter
Power	120 bhp approx.

Drivetrain
Dual-clutch semiautomatic transmission, front-wheel drive

Suspension, Wheels, and Brakes
19-in. (483-mm) wheels front and rear

Weights and Measurements

Wheelbase	97 in. (2,467 mm)
Length	151 in. (3,835 mm)
Width	68 in. (1,730 mm)
Height	57 in. (1,446 mm)

Performance

Fuel economy	78 mpg

Debut:	Los Angeles 2010
Lead designer:	Frank Saucedo
Key designer:	Niki Smart

Chevrolet Nomad (2004)

Chevrolet had introduced the Nomad station wagon, to its U.S. offerings as far back as 1955. One of the many variants of "Tri-Chevy" offered between 1955 and 1957, the Nomad had gone on to become a true icon and one of the more collectible U.S. classics. Large and luxurious, the Nomad's classic styling stood the test of time far better than many of its contemporaries, so it made sense for Chevrolet to revive the brand in 1999 with a new station-wagon car concept.

Ugly but eye-catching with its sleek design, this Nomad for the twenty-first century looked like a three-door station wagon but actually packed cool sliding rear doors on each side for easier entry and exit. However, it was ultimately doomed to be forgotten because the design wasn't especially cohesive, unlike the all-new Nomad concept of 2004.

While earlier Nomads—both concept and production—were generously proportioned, the 2004 edition was far more compact. The reason for this Nomad's size was the unexpected success of the BMW Mini in the United States; it seemed "small" no longer meant an automatic sales handicap. The Nomad was designed to appeal to drivers of any age, like the Mini—and just like that car, there was plenty of space inside despite the proportions.

Also just like the Mini, the new Nomad was designed in Great Britain, under the watchful eye of GM's design director Simon Cox, but it was built by Pininfarina in Italy, so it was a truly international effort. However, while the Nomad may have made perfect sense on so many levels, GM ultimately decided not to put it into production. Unusually, while the Nomad effectively signaled an intention to take the Chevrolet brand upmarket, GM actually went the other way and turned this division into its budget brand. And sadly, while the Nomad worked wonderfully in concept form, watering it down significantly for production would have just created a major disappointment.

Above: The original Nomad had proved to be something of a sales disaster, although it has since become a cult classic. Who knows . . . maybe this one could succeed where its predecessor failed?

Left to right: The Nomad looked great from every angle, thanks to the long hood, shallow glass house, and very clean lines.

Technology

The original Chevy Nomad concept of 1954 used the newly introduced Corvette chassis for its basis. In the same way, the 2004 concept took a new platform and used it to show what was possible. In this case, it was GM's new Kappa unit, meaning there was a turbocharged four-cylinder engine up front, which drove the rear wheels via an electronically controlled five-speed automatic transmission.

The engine packed a useful 250 brake horsepower through the use of variable engine valve timing, valve lift, and duration, which could be adjusted throughout the rev range to improve fuel economy, emissions, and performance. As such, the Nomad's power plant was significantly more powerful than was to be expected, and with the power going to the rear it was clear that driving enthusiasts were the ones being targeted. After all, in this segment it was much more usual to have the power going to the front wheels; such a configuration means not only more efficient packaging, but also lower production costs.

GM's HydraMatic transmission was also a clever design because it featured a fully automatic mode, or the driver could flick through ratios sequentially by tapping on the gear shift, a system that's become increasingly popular in recent years.

Because the Nomad was a showcase for some of GM's new production technologies and components, it wasn't the tech-fest that it might have been. Indeed, aside from some of the detailing, there was no reason why the Nomad couldn't have gone into production in this form, even if the specification was scaled back.

Top: Nomad's dash design was simplicity itself but with high-quality materials used throughout.

Middle: Most of the instrumentation was analog, but there was the odd digital display thrown in for good measure. It was all backlit in blue.

Bottom: Just like the original Nomad, the twenty-first-century edition was intended to offer a certain degree of practicality.

Opposite: Finally, a station wagon that looks sharp.

Design

Unsurprisingly, the 2004 Nomad used a variety of styling devices that directly referenced the original, iconic production car. These included the ribs set into the roof panel as well as the chrome strips on the outside of the tailgate—subtle, yet very effective.

However, this wasn't just a rehash of an earlier design, because items like the flush glazing and the integral bumpers and grille were a world away from anything made half a century earlier. So, too, were the LED lights, which were very powerful despite being extremely compact—and they looked seriously high-tech, too, when illuminated.

While the original Nomad had size on its side so it could accommodate pretty much anything you threw at it, the new one had to be more cleverly designed if it was to be practical. Toward that goal, there was a removable rear roof panel as well as a tailgate, which could be folded for the accommodation of really bulky items. To aid the stowing and removal of luggage, there was also a sliding cargo floor, so items could be pushed in and pulled out more easily.

Much more interesting than ultimate practicality, however, was the set of 20-inch (508-millimeter) wheels, which really were ridiculously oversized, but they also looked great when wrapped in ultralow profile tires. Indeed, the Nomad's design—both overall and in detail—worked wonderfully, so it's a shame that Chevrolet never to put it into production.

At a Glance

Country of Manufacture
USA/Italy

Designed in Great Britain

Engine
Front-mounted, turbocharged, four-cylinder gas

Displacement	2.2 liters
Power	250 bhp
Torque	240 lb.-ft.

Drivetrain
Five-speed sequential manual transmission, rear-wheel drive

Suspension, Wheels, and Brakes
Front suspension: Double wishbones with coil springs

Rear suspension: Double wishbones with coil springs

Brakes: Ventilated discs with twin-piston calipers front and rear

Wheels: 20 x 8½ in. (508 x 212.5 mm) alloy wheels front and rear, with 245/45 R20 Continental tires

Weights and Measurements

Wheelbase	107 in. (2,717 mm)
Length	156 in. (3,950 mm)
Width	67 in. (1,700 mm)
Height	55 in. (1,400 mm)

Debut:	Detroit 2004
Design director:	Simon Cox

Chrysler ME412 (2004)

When Chrylser unveiled its ME412 at the 2004 Detroit Motor Show, the company went to great pains to point out that this was not a concept. Instead, it was a prototype that could have been ready for the road within six months. Not only that, but the company was also seriously considering building anywhere between 10 and 2,000 examples. There was also talk of perhaps 100 cars being built each year for a couple of years—whatever happened, Chrysler really wanted to see this car hit the road. However, it never happened, of course. It may have had a halo effect and lifted the reputation of the rest of Chrylser's range, but the price was simply far too high. Trying to engineer and sell the car just wouldn't have made sense in a world that was fast becoming choked with ultraexpensive supercars that had little prospect of finding owners.

The reasoning behind the ME412 was that anything that Bugatti could do, so could Chrysler. With Bugatti having been working on the Veyron for several years, and with completion of the project not too far away, Chrysler didn't want to be left behind. The Veyron was set to offer 987 brake horsepower, but Chrysler reckoned that with "just" 850 brake horsepower, it would be able to produce a car that would give the Bugatti a run for its money in terms of top speed and acceleration.

However, Chrysler didn't have the resources to get the ME412 into production. Its more mainstream models were struggling, so its designers and engineers had to work flat out to try to make them competitive. It was a great tragedy, because as a result, the ME412 is one of the all-time great "what might have been" stories.

Above: If ever there was an "if only" concept, it's this one. Chrysler fully intended to put the car into limited production, but it wasn't to be.

Left to right: With its cab-forward stance, the ME412 featured classic mid-engine supercar styling—and that was one hefty engine that had to be accommodated, because it was a 6-liter V12 unit.

Technology

To offer such astonishingly high levels of performance, the ME412 had to be fitted with something pretty special in the engine stakes. The basis of the power plant was the AMG-produced 365 ci (5,980 cc) V12 power plant that was available in various Mercedes models. Capable of developing around 600 brake horsepower when used elsewhere, Chrysler's engineers needed to beef it up considerably if it was to offer serious competition to the Bugatti Veyron. Toward that goal, no fewer than four turbochargers were bolted onto it to produce a completely insane 142 brake horsepower per liter.

Of course, it's relatively easy to generate huge amounts of power from an engine, and also to produce massive amounts of specific power (horsepower per liter), but the trick is to keep everything tractable at low revs and road speeds. With modern electronics, this didn't prove too much of a problem; what was perhaps more impressive was the peak torque of 850 lb.-ft., which was available from just 2,500 rpm.

If keeping the engine tractable at low speeds seemed like a hurdle, it was nothing compared with getting all that power down without drama. A rear-wheel-drive layout was used instead, which Chrysler claimed could put the power down without lighting up the rear tires every time the throttle was dabbed. The transmission, built by Ricardo, was fitted with seven speeds and featured a pair of clutches to enable faster gear changes than usual.

The seven-speed Ricardo Double Clutch Transmission was developed specifically for the ME412 concept. Fitted with the latest double wet-clutch technology and electronic control, the transmission was strong and capable of swapping ratios in lightning-quick time. The transmission was so well engineered that it was able to deliver uninterrupted torque to the rear wheels with shift times of just 200 milliseconds—which may not have been quite as quick as contemporary Formula One cars, but it was better than anything available for road use.

Opposite, top: One of the criticisms leveled at virtually all of Chrysler's cars is low interior quality. Not here!

Opposite, middle: Everywhere you looked there were premium-quality materials, with aluminum and leather all over the place.

Opposite, bottom: It was becoming fashionable to incorporate a flat-base steering wheel into supercars by this point.

Above: The ME412's engine was huge but beautiful.

Left: Few contemporary supercars could offer the visual drama of the ME412; this was a car designed for maximum visual impact.

Right, above: Chrysler was eager to promote its American roots when promoting the ME412; it was effectively giving the Italians the finger.

Right, below: The outside of the ME412 was also littered with gorgeouss details, not least of all the fabulous multispoke alloy wheels.

Opposite: The ME412's dramatic design produced a very low drag coefficient for a supercar.

Design

The year before the ME412 was unveiled, the Dodge Tomahawk concept was revealed to the world. One of the most insane concepts ever devised, trying to top the Tomahawk was always going to be difficult—and in reality, the ME412 didn't even come close. However, as a mid-engine hypercar, it was dramatic, but with the car being supposedly almost production ready, the designers had to be reined in.

The body shell was as high-tech as they come, being produced of carbon fiber around an aluminum honeycomb tub. For a supercar it was slippery, too, with a drag coefficient of 0.36. However, with almost 250 miles (400 kilometers) per hour on the cards, there needed to be some pretty neat design features to cope with such high speeds. There was a front of the car-mounted splitter to increase downforce plus an integral rear diffuser to reduce lift and provide additional rear downforce. Formations in the belly pan forward of each wheel reduced lift, while the decklid's rear ski-slope formation boosted rear downforce even further.

The car's potential was also given away by its cabin, which featured its exposed carbon fiber body tub throughout. However, it wasn't all stripped bare; the sports seats were trimmed with leather, while there was also a premium sound system plus climate control. More important, however, because Chrysler fully intended to put the ME412 into limited production, it had taken the time to ensure that its cabin was usable and comfortable—unlike many of its more compromised potential rivals.

At a Glance

Country of Manufacture
USA

Engine
Midmounted, quad-turbo, gas V12

Displacement	365 ci (5,980 cc)
Power	850 bhp
Torque	850 lb.-ft.

Drivetrain
Seven-speed manual transmission, rear-wheel drive

Suspension, Wheels, and Brakes
Front suspension: Double wishbones with driver-adjustable pushrod spring/shock absorber units

Rear suspension: Double wishbones with driver-adjustable pushrod spring/shock absorber units

Brakes: 15-in. (381-mm) ventilated carbon discs all around

19 x 10 alloy wheels at the front with 265/35ZR19 tires

20 x 12.5 alloy wheels at the rear with 335/30ZR20 tires

Weights and Measurements

Curb weight	2,888 lb. (1,310 kg)
Length	179 in. (4,542 mm)
Width	79 in. (2,000 mm)
Height	45 in. (1,140 mm)

Performance

0–62 mph	3.0 seconds
Top speed	248 mph (399 km/h)
Debut:	Detroit 2004

Citroën GT (2008)

There was a time when Citroën was renowned for its cutting-edge design and its fearlessness at embracing new technologies. It was this approach that saw the wonderful Traction Avant launched in 1934, the sensational DS in 1955, and a string of innovative machines, such as the 2CV, GS, and CX, as well. However, Citroën has also gone bust twice, so being innovative isn't always as financially rewarding as you might hope.

With its design and engineering watered down significantly by the 1990s, Citroën was producing cars that could have worn the badges of just about any conservative mainstream carmaker. What it needed to do was rediscover its soul. It took until the arrival of the DS3 in 2009 for Citroën to prove that it was finally capable of producing distinctive production cars once again, even if it had built a string of great concepts along the way.

One of the most sensational—indeed, by far the most outrageous—was the GT, officially known as the somewhat pretentious GTbyCitroën. Seemingly parachuted in from a parallel universe, the GT came about thanks to a partnership between Citroën and Polyphony, creators of the *Gran Turismo* driving game. The latter wanted something seriously special for its fifth edition of the iconic game's franchise, and Citroën was happy to oblige with a car that borrowed nothing from its existing model lineup—but it did prove that its design studios had plenty to offer when allowed off the leash.

As a result, despite a massive array of supercars already being on sale, Citroën was inundated with requests from potential buyers, demanding that the GT be put into production. Within less than a year of the GT concept being unveiled, Citroën then announced that it would be building a very limited number of road-going editions for sale. Priced at well over a million Euros ($1,230,000) apiece, just half a dozen would be made, with a carbon-fiber construction and all the crazy exterior details still intact. Despite Citroën's assurance that the car would make limited production, things then went strangely quiet . . .

Above: The GT was a huge leap into the unknown for Citroën, which claimed it would build six road-going cars . . . but they never happened.

Left to right: It's easy to see why Citroën didn't build any road-going examples of the GT; it would have been incredibly expensive to build, thanks to the complicated construction.

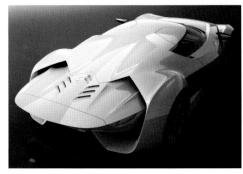

Technology

Remember that the GT started out as a virtual car, designed for only driving games. The reality came later. When the GT was unveiled in 2008, few details were revealed about the car's power plant or drivetrain. As a result, despite its extremely high-tech appearance, just about all of the GT's technical details were assumed; with this car, Citroën's focus was on the design, not the details of how the thing would work.

What Citroën did reveal was that the GT was powered by a fuel cell; keeping in mind that production fuel cells were still thought to be several years away at this point, not least because of a lack of refueling infrastructure, the GT clearly was the stuff of dreams. With a fuel cell generating electricity, which then drives electric motors, the GT could have featured drive to only the rear wheels or to all four. More probable, however, the car would be something between the two: an adjustable setup that would have varied the amount of torque going to each corner, depending on the grip available—or perhaps even a fully adjustable system, so the driver could set up the car's dynamics to suit the occasion.

Because the GT's power train was so far into the future, the inclusion of a conventional internal combustion engine would have been necessary, but it didn't have to look any less sensational or go any less quickly. Indeed, with a 700 brake horsepower V8 mounted in the middle, the GT could easily have touched the 200 miles (320 kilometers) per hour that its amazing lines promised.

Top: The interior was no less mind-blowing than the exterior. This was a design that offered the originality of Citroën's past models.

Middle: With its reclining seating position, the GT's occupants were left in no doubt to the type of car they were in: a major-league supercar.

Bottom: With such amazing detailing, it's probably just as well that Citroën never productionised the GT; a watered-down version would have been a tragedy.

Opposite: The GT's interior gave a full luxury experience not often felt in the race cars its exterior emulated.

Design

Citroën attempted to make the GT look even more dynamic by painting the front white but the rear gray, with a continuous fade between the two along the car's length. Intriguingly, according to Citroën, the rear end was oversized, made exaggeratedly long "in order to create an effect of retinal persistence"—it's that designer technobabble again.

What was much easier to understand were the 21-inch (533-millimeter) diamond-effect aluminum wheels, the car's gull-wing doors, the oversize rear end with adjustable spoiler, and the gaping air intakes and flat underside, all of which were taken straight from the racetrack.

Meanwhile, the high-tech interior featured a darker color theme with two padded racing seats finished in black leather and fitted with four-point harnesses. The dark leather, along with copper and steel touches inside the cabin and a low-slung driving position, created an opulent environment, while important onboard data was displayed via a red LED head-up display, allowing drivers to maintain focus on the track ahead.

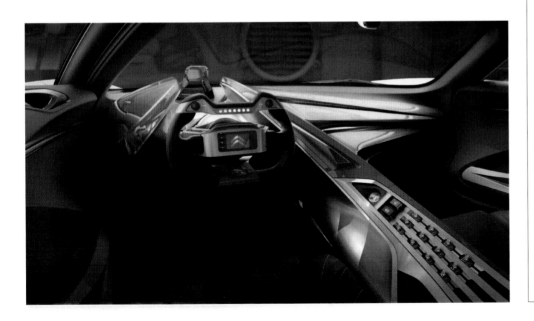

At a Glance

Country of Manufacture
France/Japan

Engine
Midmounted hydrogen fuel cell

Power   780 bhp

Drivetrain
Four electric motors, one at each wheel, to provide four-wheel drive

Suspension, Wheels, and Brakes
21-in. (533-mm) alloy wheels, front and rear

Weights and Measurements

Curb weight	3,086 lb. (1,400 kg)
Length	195 in. (4,960 mm)
Width	82 in. (2,080 mm)
Height	43 in. (1,090 mm)

Performance

0–62 mph	Under 5 seconds
Top speed	200 mph (322 km/h) approx.

Debut:	Paris 2008
Designer:	Takumi Yamamoto

Citroën Lacoste (2010)

For most people in 2010, life had become all too serious. That was Citroën's contention anyway, and with the Lacoste, its aim was to do something about it—to inject some fun into peoples' lives by producing a car that was fresh and innovative yet still decently usable. After years of so-so design, Citroën had finally rediscovered its mojo around this time, and the Lacoste was proof that, once again, people might buy a one of the company's cars to stand out from the crowd—and not just because they wanted cheap transport.

When it was unveiled, Citroën claimed that the Lacoste "alluded to leisure and pleasure, taking a simplified, no-nonsense approach to motoring—without forgetting refinement—and transporting passengers to a lighter, fresher world." While it would be easy to see that as marketing hype, it spelled out very clearly where Citroën positioned this fun-loving concept.

That position was somewhere close to the Mini Moke of the 1960s, so while the Lacoste didn't major on performance, it was intended to provide some kind of driving thrills. Like the Moke, the Lacoste offered a back-to-basics approach that put fun above everything else, largely thanks to offering an exposure to the elements that was missing from most open-topped cars of the time. By keeping its weight to a minimum, the Lacoste also promised the type of agility not seen since the Moke.

You didn't have to drive the Lacoste for it to raise a smile; just looking at it was enough to have those laughter muscles exercised like mad, and let's face it—you can't say that about many cars of the twenty-first century.

Above: In plan view, it's easy to see just how neatly packaged the Lacoste was, with most of the car's length given to its four passengers.

Left to right: Although it looks as though there's no weather protection, in reality there's a rain-activated curtain built into that longitudinal roll bar—a very neat solution.

Technology

The Lacoste was never meant to be a technological tour de force; indeed, one of its key points was that it featured as little technology as possible. This was meant to be a stripped-out fun car at its heart. That's not to say it was completely devoid of innovation, with the dashboard's large-pixel information display being the highlight. While this didn't look especially impressive—it was a reference to the original video games of the 1980s—it was actually a lot more high-tech than it looked. This information display provided details of the car's speed and other functions, while also flashing oversize icons in place of the more usual warning lights.

It was around this time that most concepts—and, indeed, many production cars—were using much more compact lighting than had been the case in the past. As a result, the front and rear lights of the Lacoste were very discreet, to the point that they were barely noticeable until they were illuminated, which would have been impossible just a few years before.

Although Citroën released images of the Lacoste being driven—which suggested it was a fully functioning prototype—the company didn't reveal any details about its power train. While the Lacoste could have packed a gasoline/electric drivetrain, it's more probable that any production car would have been either fully electric or powered simply by a conventional internal combustion engine. Either way, the car would have looked sensational.

Top: The single-spoke steering wheel was a direct nod to Citroën's past; many of its cars from the 1950s, 1960s, and 1970s featured one.

Middle: The simplicity of the dash was all too apparent—until the complicated display lit up. It was integrated into the dashboard itself.

Bottom: The Lacoste was another one of those concepts that looked great no matter where you stood to look at it. It would have made a great fun car.

Design

The Lacoste made no pretence at being practical. This was a car designed for having fun in the sunshine, and if it was pelting down with rain—well, you just had to have less fun. Probably. But you didn't have to get soaked through, because while the Lacoste looked as though it was roofless—aside from the central spine that ran along its length—there was actually some basic protection available from the elements. When rain was detected, the roof would pop out from this spine, although the sides of the car were still left open. However, by making this roof from a translucent yellow material, whatever the weather was doing, the Lacoste's interior was bathed in warm light.

By leaving the sides of the Lacoste fully open, entry and exit couldn't have been easier, but the front doors were replaced by cutouts that would have given the health and safety nannies palpitations. Access to the rear seats was just as simple (or dangerous), with passengers simply jumping onto the rear bench, which could be slid into the trunk so bulky items could be transported more easily.

Indeed, the Lacoste was aimed at those with active lifestyles, which is why it could also be fitted with specially designed sports equipment, such as tennis racquets, golf clubs, skis, a surfboard, or a bike, with owners deciding on the theme of their weekends.

As Citroën put it, the Lacoste combined elements from the various worlds of motoring, fashion, and sport, taking stylistic references from all three. The cabin featured countless storage areas for extra practicality, while the seats were oversewn in white cotton, the weave closely resembling that of a polo shirt—an iconic Lacoste design. Building on this theme, the seat belt anchorage points featured "necklines" like a polo shirt, while the seats were covered in robust, ropelike cotton.

At a Glance

Country of Manufacture
France

Engine
Front-mounted, normally aspirated three-cylinder gas

Displacement	61 ci (998 cc)
Power	68 bhp
Torque	69 lb.-ft.

Drivetrain
Five-speed manual transmission, front-wheel drive

Suspension, Wheels, and Brakes
Unavailable

Weights and Measurements

Wheelbase	91 in. (2,300 mm)
Length	136 in. (3,450 mm)
Width	71 in. (1,800 mm)
Height	60 in. (1,520 mm)
Debut:	Paris 2010

Dodge Zeo (2008)

Dodge didn't know it, but when its Zeo concept was unveiled at the 2008 Detroit Motor Show, the company was about to go to hell and back. That's because while the Zeo, or Zero Emissions Operation concept, was bristling with social conscience, it was a case of too little, too late. Within months the enormous Chrysler group, which Dodge is a part of, filed for bankruptcy. However, the company received government protection, along with billions of dollars' worth of loans, which would enable it to rebuild itself before finally being sold to the Fiat Group.

Until this point, Dodge had been about XXL SUVs, unashamed muscle cars, and oversize pickups; you had to search in vain for anything within its range that was truly energy efficient. However, as the era of cheap fuel came to an end and a global recession struck, car buyers around the world switched to smaller, cheaper cars that put fuel efficiency first. So, while Dodge was unveiling the Zeo, its factories were still busy churning out huge, thirsty trucks and sedans. These were vehicles that a decreasing number of buyers wanted—or could afford.

The Zeo aimed to show that Dodge could be environmentally aware—and most crucially, it was built to demonstrate that being green didn't have to mean being dull. Here was a car that looked sensational and was capable of accelerating at a breakneck pace, yet it could be run on renewable energies, such as solar or wind power. And this wasn't at the expense of practicality, because there was seating for four—even if those in the back were ideally amputees under five years old. It showed at least that Dodge was making an effort to embrace the concept of efficiency—something it had never really had to bother with before. Welcome to the new world order.

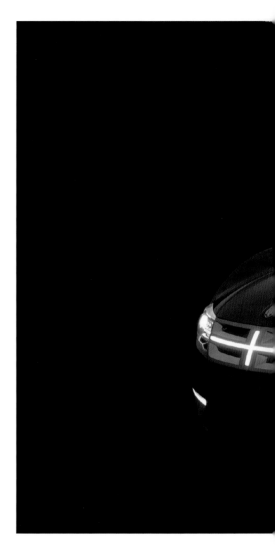

Above: This wasn't how electric cars were supposed to look. The Zeo didn't look like the worthy designs that were typical of contemporary electric cars.

Left to right: While the Zeo looked great from the front and also the rear, it seemed as though two designs had been joined together, with the car ending a little too abruptly.

Technology

The use of pure electric power for the Zeo meant there was no internal combustion engine of any kind. Keep in mind that there was no mainstream electric car available in the United States at this point and only conversions in Europe, so you can get a sense of the magnitude of Dodge's task in convincing buyers that the Zeo might be a viable proposition as everyday transport.

In a bid to make the Zeo as viable as possible, Dodge fitted it with lithium-ion batteries that gave a claimed range of at least 250 miles (400 kilometers). Such figures are invariably overoptimistic, however, and especially so if owners regularly used the available performance. This was a car that was capable of beating Dodge's regular performance sedans on the drag strip. By using all of the available performance, the Zeo could be accelerated from a standing start to 62 miles (100 kilometers) per hour in just 5.8 seconds—the kind of acceleration that would normally take a large-capacity gasoline V8 to achieve.

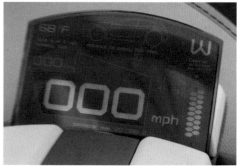

Because there was no internal combustion engine onboard to top up the batteries, they had to be recharged using a main outlet. However, part of the technology package fitted included regenerative braking, so every time the car slowed the batteries would be topped up. Still, there was little chance of anyone managing to squeeze 250 miles (400 kilometers) out of the Zeo, unless it was driven downhill for 150 (240) of them.

Top: For a four-seater coupé, the use of scissor doors perhaps wasn't the best idea, but they certainly added to the visual drama.

Middle: The Zeo was meant to be a cutting-edge eco car, so its cabin was filled with cutting-edge displays to emphasize its modernity.

Bottom: Instead of door-mounted mirrors, there were cameras that relayed images to the dash-mounted display. They were more aerodynamic than mirrors.

Opposite: The Zeo's exterior was painted a bright "supercar orange" to highlight its contoured bodywork.

Design

A four-seater electric car might sound like a recipe for boredom on wheels, but that didn't stop Dodge from creating an eco-mobile that looked nothing less than sensational. Perhaps its background of building profligate supercars helped here. Whatever it was, the Zeo didn't look like a tree hugger's dream.

The retina-frying orange paintwork made sure that nobody missed the Zeo. Its heavily contoured bodywork helped to increase visibility, too. The A-pillars consisted of a single gentle curve from the base of the windshield right to the back of the car, with the windshield doing exactly the same—it started out as a windshield but became a glass roof in one continuous sweep. And just like all concepts worth a second glance, the doors featured a scissor action; after all, why keep things simple when you can maximize the drama?

Just in case there was a chance of anybody not noticing the Zeo, it was also fitted with 23-inch (584-millimeter) alloy wheels, pushed right out to the corners to maximize interior space. That interior was just as inviting as the exterior, thanks to the use of high-quality materials, plus a full-length sunroof that really opened things up. There was ample space for two up front, but those in the rear were going to find things tight—hence the 2+2 billing.

At a Glance

Country of Manufacture
USA

Engine
Rear-mounted 200 kW electric motor with regenerative braking

Displacement	64 kWh lithium-ion battery pack
Power	272 bhp

Drivetrain
Automatic transmission, rear-wheel drive

Suspension, Wheels, and Brakes
Front suspension: Double wishbones with coil springs

Rear suspension: Double wishbones with coil springs

Front tires: 225/40 R23

Rear tires: 255/40 R23

Weights and Measurements

Curb weight	2,650 lb. (1,202 kg)
Wheelbase	110 in. (2,792 mm)
Length	173 in. (4,390 mm)
Width	77 in. (1,944 mm)
Height	51 in. (1,290 mm)

Performance

0–62 mph	5.7 seconds
Top speed	130 mph (209 km/h)
Range	250 miles (400 km)

Debut:	Detroit 2008
Exterior designer:	Bill Zheng

Dodge M80 (2002)

Ever since it had embraced muscle cars wholeheartedly in the 1960s, Dodge and its parent company, the Chrysler Group, had produced cars that would make eco warriors weep. So the M80 fit in perfectly with a brand that had little, if any, social conscience.

Except all was not what it seemed. In isolation, the M80 looked like just another bad-boy SUV intent on destroying the planet, but it wasn't like that. The M80 was actually meant to herald the start of a new generation of more compact, frugal, and affordable SUVs from America. However, despite its relatively diminutive proportions, the M80 was intended to be just as tough and versatile as its bigger stablemates; as Dodge put it, the M80 offered "surf to snow" capabilities and was an authentic job-rated vehicle.

The M80 came about thanks to designer John Opfer, who grew up in California and could be at the beach within an hour or on the ski slopes if he drove for an hour in the opposite direction. His aim was to create a leisure vehicle that would be equally at home in either situation. Aimed at youngsters who wanted to get away from it all, the M80 ideally could transport two adventurers, complete with all their gear, to far-flung places in a bid to escape the city for the weekend. But during the week, the M80 would be just as at home negotiating city streets; while it didn't look much like a compact SUV, that's exactly what the M80 was.

Above: There was no mistaking where the M80 originated from with those Tonka Toy looks. This pickup was clearly American.

Left to right: It's hard to get a sense of scale from these shots of the M80. While it looks huge, it was actually much smaller and more frugal than U.S. car buyers were used to.

Technology

American cars are famed for their low-tech approach, and the M80 was no different. By keeping the M80 light on the tech, its weight and cost could be kept down, while the reliability would be top-notch. As a result, you'd look in vain for evidence of novel propulsion systems, cutting-edge safety features, or driver assistance systems. Instead, the M80 was utterly conventional in its engineering and technology because it used components throughout that were tried and tested.

In the front of the car was the 3.7-liter gasoline V6 that would soon become very familiar to a mass of Chrysler Group customers, because it would be fitted to other models, such as the Voyager, Sebring, and Nitro. Despite its relatively generous capacity and the M80's low curb weight of just 2,500 pounds (1,134 kilograms), it was disappointing that a top speed of only 100 miles (160 kilometers) per hour or so was offered—this was never intended to be a speed machine.

As you'd expect of such a go-anywhere vehicle, there was permanent four-wheel drive with a 4x4 transfer case to keep the car moving when things got tricky. A five-speed manual transmission completed the picture, and as if to underline the M80's utilitarian nature, it featured nothing more sophisticated than a live rear axle suspended by leaf springs. Electronically controlled suspension with height adjustment? Nah—that was for wimps.

Top: In typical concept-car fashion, the cabin was stuffed with aluminum detailing to emphasize its high-quality nature.

Middle: Despite the relatively luxurious materials used, the cabin still focused on utility—it was almost a hose-down cabin for those off-road excursions.

Bottom: There was seating for just two, but if somebody wanted to travel solo there was extra versatility available with the folding passenger seat.

Opposite: Here, the M80 is shown in its natural environment: on the beach with a surfer.

Design

You'd search in vain for evidence of futuristic styling where the M80 was concerned; the inspiration behind it was a series of classic SUVs that included the 1939 TC and 1941 WC trucks from Dodge's past. As a result, there were exposed front and rear wheel arches along with a narrow-body design evocative of postwar trucks.

To emphasize its tough nature, the wheel arches were black plastic instead of body-colored; there were also no bumpers, so those wheel arches would have to work hard for their living. At first glance, the M80 looked minimalist, but actually there were plenty of cool design flourishes if you took a closer look. Each front fender incorporated an aluminum vent, and the side mirrors were beautifully made from aluminum. Indeed, most of the exterior details were finished in alloy, including the door handles, fuel filler, and grille—the latter featuring the trademark Dodge crosshair.

At the back, there were dual exhausts and a wonderfully retro tailgate with Dodge branding stamped into it. What was less obvious was the locker mounted on each side just ahead of the rear wheel; it was an innovative touch that boosted practicality and security. It was the load bay that offered the greatest practicality, however. Covered by its own plastic cover to keep prying eyes at bay, the window between the cab and the load bay could also be flipped up for easy access or to store especially long loads.

At a Glance

Country of Manufacture
USA

Engine
Front-mounted, normally aspirated gas V6

Displacement	3.7 liters
Power	210 bhp
Torque	235 lb.-ft.

Drivetrain
Five-speed manual transmission, four-wheel drive

Suspension, Wheels, and Brakes
Front suspension: Independent with double wishbones, torsion bars, shock absorbers, and anti-roll bar

Rear supension: Live axle with leaf springs and shock absorbers

Wheels: 9x20 front and rear

Tires: 265/50 R20 Goodyears

Weights and Measurements

Curb weight	2,500 lb. (1,134 kg)
Wheelbase	112 in. (2,845 mm)
Length	166 in. (4,229 mm)
Width	64 in. (1,631 mm)
Height	66 in. (1,687 mm)

Performance

0–62 mph	8 seconds
Top speed	100 mph (160 km/h) approx.

Debut:	Detroit 2002
Designer:	John Opfer
Design director:	Dave McKinnon

Ferrari Pinin (1980)

While some carmakers churn out one concept after another, Ferrari has never built one itself—or at least not in-house. Instead, coachbuilders, such as Bertone and Pininfarina, create visions of what Ferrari could build. The result is concepts such as Bertone's 308GT Rainbow of 1976 along with Pininfarina's Rossa of 2000. Much more interesting, however, was the Pinin, unveiled by Pininfarina at the 1980 Turin salon, to celebrate Pininfarina's fiftieth birthday.

While the fact that this concept was billed as a Ferrari was interesting enough, it was especially fascinating that it was a four-door sedan. Until this point, Ferrari had never put into production anything so mundane as a sedan car, although it had done several four-seater (or 2+2) coupés, such as the 330GT and 365GTC/4. But then, of course, this was no ordinary four-door sedan.

Besides, why should the idea of building a sedan be so crazy, even for a super carmaker? Many years later, Porsche strayed from its natural habitat to build an off-roader, as did Maserati. However, in more than six decades of car production, Ferrari still has never offered anything so mundane as a four-door sedan in its production line—although its FF station wagon of 2011 was more prosaic, on paper, than anything it had built before.

If Ferrari had ever been tempted to build a car for families, the Pinin would surely have been deserving of the Prancing Horse badge; this was one cutting-edge car when it was first shown in 1980. While performance was the order of the day, thanks to a 5-liter flat-12 engine up front, there was also luxury. So far Ferrari has stayed with two doors, but with Porsche and Aston Martin both building four-door sedans, and Lamborghini having displayed a four-seater sedan concept that could yet be put into production, maybe it's only a matter of time . . .

Above: From this angle it's easy to see that the Pinin's roof line was too high—either that or the window line was set too low.

Left to right: The idea of a Ferrari sedan was too radical, which is why the Pinin never saw the light of day as a production car. Even now, Ferrari has never offered a four-door sedan.

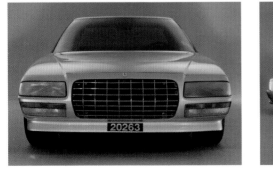

Technology

Mechanically, there was little to excite where the Pinin was concerned. The 12-cylinder engine of the ultrafast 512 Boxer was mounted up front, while the rest of the running gear— including the suspension and transmission—was also taken from the fastest car produced by Ferrari at the time.

Its eye-catching exterior design details were far more innovative, with the front and rear lights featuring the latest technologies. Up front, the headlights incorporated multireflectors to produce a much brighter light at night; until now, most headlights were almost as tall as they were wide. However, with the Pinin, much lower, sleeker lighting was possible, which kicked out more light than conventional rivals. Meanwhile, the rear lights were also much brighter than usual, yet when they weren't illuminated it was hard to tell that they were light units at all.

The interior looked just as high-tech as the exterior, thanks to the extensive use of LED instrumentation. As a result, until the engine was fired up, the displays all remained gloss black—at which point they'd light up like Christmas trees. A computer provided information on fuel consumption, average speed and distance, and a countdown in miles and time for a preprogramed destination. There was plenty of luxury, too; rear seat passengers got a telephone and their own radio complete with headsets, while climate control ensured the cabin temperature could be maintained regardless of how hot or cold it was outside.

Top: With that brown leather and suede trim, this could only be an Italian car of the 1970s, except the Pinin was actually unveiled in 1980 . . .

Middle: The age of the microchip was virtually upon us at this stage, which is why concepts from this period started to become stuffed with electronics— usually nonfunctional.

Bottom: In true Ferrari fashion, there was plenty of power available, thanks to the legendary flat-12 engine.

Opposite: For a relatively boxy car of 1980, the Pinin had enough curves to keep the drag down.

Design

The key thing about the Pinin was its configuration. As the first four-door sedan to carry Ferrari badges, designers faced a challenge in incorporating traditional Ferrari styling cues, although this was intended to be a concept that looked forward instead of back. As such, aside from Ferrari's familiar egg-crate grille, there was little to give away the fact that this car wore those hallowed prancing horse badges.

The only other obvious Ferrari reference was the choice of wheel; the five-spoke alloys offered a nod to Ferrari's production cars, but for the Pinin there was a twist—literally. Each spoke was twisted to turn it into a blade, which was eye-catching while also being functional, because the blades fed cooling air to the brake discs.

The most striking thing about the car, however, was its flush glazing—it would be another few years before Audi famously introduced its ultraslippery 100 sedan, with an advertising campaign constructed around the fact that it featured a drag coefficient of just 0.30.

To accentuate the Pinin's slippery shape, the glass was heavily tinted so that the pillars could be disguised; it was meant to look as though there was one continuous sheet of glass all around. Meanwhile, the windshield wipers were hidden when not in use—a common design trick nowadays—but something that was unheard of when the car was unveiled in 1980.

At a Glance

Country of Manufacture
Italy

Engine
Front-mounted, normally aspirated gas V12

Displacement	301 ci (4,942 cc)
Power	360 bhp
Torque	332 lb.-ft.

Drivetrain
Five-speed manual transmission, rear-wheel drive

Suspension, Handling, and Braking
Front suspension: Double wishbones with coil springs

Rear suspension: Double wishbones with coil springs

Ventilated disc brakes all around

Weights and Measurements

Wheelbase	108 in. (2,750 mm)
Length	190 in. (4,830 mm)
Width	72 in. (1,820 mm)
Height	52 in. (1,310 mm)

Performance

0–62 mph	6.0 seconds approx.
Top speed	180 mph (290 km/h) approx.

Debut:	Turin 1980
Designer:	Leonardo Fioravanti

Fiat Oltre (2005)

Most of Fiat's concepts over the years have been small cars that are all about clever packaging—after all, this is where Fiat has traditionally excelled, with iconic models, such as the Topolino, 500, Panda, and Uno. Indeed, when teetering on the brink in 2008, it was the reborn 500 that proved to be Fiat's savior. Sure it was priced a bit high for a small Fiat, but those ultrachic lines and much-improved build quality were well worth the extra cash.

Before Fiat went through its dark days, it unveiled a concept that was nothing less than insane: the Oltre. It seemed that the company was just following the then-current fashion for overblown monsters that used as much fuel as possible, despite the Oltre being born into an otherwise eco-conscious age. Doing its best to take on the Hummer at its own game, the Oltre was a huge, boxy off-roader that looked as though it had come straight from the heart of a war zone.

However, as is often the case with concepts, all was not what it seemed. The Oltre was based on Iveco's LMV (light multirole vehicle) military off-road machine, so it was hardly a clean-sheet design for Fiat. The LMV, an impressive piece of military hardware, later became a favorite of armies around the globe, thanks to its combination of toughness, go-anywhere abilities, and flexibility—there were versions capable of taking between five and seven people. The Oltre itself, however, was capable of accommodating just five, albeit in considerably more luxury than the standard car could provide.

With a crew cab as the basis, the Oltre could carry people as well as cargo—no less than three tons of cargo in fact, which meant that by the time the Oltre was fully laden, it could weigh up to seven tons. Very eco-aware . . .

Above: If you saw this picture in isolation, you'd assume it was of a model car. The Oltre looked more like a parody of an off-roader than an example of the real thing.

Left to right: It didn't matter what angle you viewed the Oltre from—this was one seriously ugly car. And those wheels looked just ridiculous.

Technology

While many concepts are technology showcases, the Oltre was all about mobility. As a result, the focus was on technologies that would enable the car to go anywhere—so if you wanted a cabin filled with the latest high-tech gadgetry, you'd have to look elsewhere.

That's not to say the Oltre wasn't interesting technically; any vehicle developed for a military application tends to be intriguing, if not necessarily groundbreaking. In this case, the key technologies were in the transmission, which was a permanent four-wheel-drive system that incorporated three locking differentials. Allowing optimal grip in all conditions, Fiat claimed the Oltre could tackle a lateral gradient of up to 40 percent, along with a longitudinal gradient of up to 80 percent—pretty phenomenal!

Despite weighing up to 7 tons when fully laden, the Oltre was fitted with a four-cylinder turbodiesel engine that displaced just 3 liters. However, a variable-geometry turbo and intercooler along with common rail fuel delivery meant there was a huge amount of flexibility offered, if not necessarily all that much outright grunt.

Indeed, the power plant was capable of generating just 185 brake horsepower, but there was, nevertheless, a useful 336 lb.-ft. of torque available. Fiat reckoned the Oltre was capable of over 81 miles (130 kilometers) per hour but you can bet those figures weren't for a car tipping the scales at 7 tons.

Top: Despite its working roots, the Oltre's interior was designed with bling in mind—just like its exterior.

Middle: The blue-and-white color theme of the cabin was an extension of the colors used for the exterior; subtle, they weren't.

Bottom: There's only so much you can do to beautify the cabin of a car originally designed for military off-roading . . .

Design

From any angle you'd be hard put to call the Oltre handsome. Indeed, however you looked at it, this was an ugly beast that didn't really make a lot of sense. To start with, it was a no-holds-barred full-size SUV designed for tackling the most inhospitable terrain imaginable, yet it was fitted with enormous chromed wheels shod in low-profile tires. Perfect for rappers and football stars, but definitely not for invading armies.

However, despite an excess of bling, it was surprisingly functional because the ground clearance was a generous 20 inches (500 millimeters), which should have enabled just about any terrain to be crossed. Indeed, Fiat claimed that a 33-inch-deep (850-milimeter) ford could be traversed—or if extension pipes were added to the intake and exhaust, it was possible for the Oltre to wade through water an impressive 5 feet (1.5 meters) deep.

The exterior styling was definitely an acquired taste, with the front and rear fenders being heavily cut away, leaving much of the running gear exposed. Fiat reckoned the car's design was "exuberant," which was an understatement. Amusingly, Fiat also claimed the Oltre's door handles were flush fitting so they wouldn't get in the way during off-road maneuvers!

Exterior detailing, such as the twin antennae, roof bars, sun visor, and roof-mounted spot lights gave the Oltre a lifestyle feel, mixed with a little luxury, along with a healthy dose of practicality. This was reinforced by the side steps so beloved by superstylish young moms in their Beverly Hills–bound 4x4s. Indeed, if there was ever a car designed for urban one-upmanship—and for giving environmentalists palpitations—it was the Fiat Oltre.

At a Glance

Country of Manufacture
Italy

Engine
Front-mounted, turbocharged four-cylinder diesel

Displacement	3 liters
Power	182 bhp
Torque	336 lb.-ft.

Drivetrain
Six-speed automatic transmission, four-wheel drive

Suspension, Wheels, and Brakes
Front suspension: Independent with double wishbones and coil springs

Rear suspension: Independent with double wishbones and coil springs

Tires: Pirelli Scorpion Zero Asimmetrico 315/40R26 XL (extra load) front and rear

Weights and Measurements
Curb weight	7 tons (6,350 kg)
Wheelbase	127 in. (3,230 mm)
Length	192 in. (4,870 mm)
Width	87 in. (2,200 mm)
Height	81 in. (2,050 mm)

Performance
Top speed	81 mph (210 km/h)
Range	300 miles (483 km)
Debut:	Bologna 2005

Ford 24.7 (2000)

Most people think of their cars as mere transport, while others consider them a ticket to freedom. Some love driving their cars, but few would think their ride was capable of better organizing their lives. After all, that's what day planners are for; you're either organized or you're not. That wasn't what Ford reckoned, however, when it introduced the 24.7 concept; the company claimed this was a car that was capable of helping owners to manage their time more effectively than ever before. Hmm, right . . .

Unlike most concepts, which are unveiled in a single form, Ford created no fewer than three 24.7 variants, including a pickup truck, an SUV, and a coupé. Each was intended to provide owners with access to information, people, and places 24 hours a day and seven days a week—hence the name.

The three different variations on the 24.7 theme were each designed for different lifestyles, but all featured the same technologies and design themes. The 24.7 wagon was intended to be the ideal family vehicle that blurred the boundaries between the traditional station wagon and a conventional SUV. The 24.7 pickup, meanwhile, was ready for any user adventure; it could be packed with gear and driven into the mountains or onto the beach, and would be perfectly at home in the city as well. However, for those who rarely escaped the city, the 24.7 coupé was designed to provide perfect urban transportation. These variations were all very well, but you can't help thinking that Ford missed the mark by not coming up with a single vehicle that could do all these things.

Above: Just like the Oltre on the preceding pages, the 24.7 looks more like the kind of thing a child would play with.

Left to right: The boxy design looked incredibly simple—just like a child would draw—but once one delved deeper, it actually proved to be complex.

Technology

The 24.7 was built in conjunction with technology provider Visteon, so it had cutting-edge features. Indeed, it featured three of Visteon's then-latest advancements: voice technology, voice activated reconfigurable projected image display, and an advanced lighting system.

Predictably, voice technology allowed drivers to set controls and make phone calls while keeping their hands on the wheel and their eyes on the road. Used in conjunction with the vehicle's onboard navigation system, it included an in-vehicle Internet browser that allowed drivers to verbally retrieve weather information, road conditions, or other information. Intriguingly, Visteon claimed that its voice-activation system could understand English, French, German, Italian, Japanese, and Spanish, including multiple dialects and accents.

Then there was the reconfigurable projected image display, a voice-activated display that was a smart alternative to a more conventional instrument display, because it gave drivers the ability to customize the dashboard by changing the layout of the various instruments with simple voice commands.

Meanwhile, Visteon's latest breakthrough lighting technology was also incorporated: white and red LED lamps. These illuminated instantly, could last the life of the vehicle, allowed for much tighter packaging, and consumed a fraction of the power that traditional halogen lamps required; since the appearance of the 24.7, such technology has become widespread in mainstream production cars.

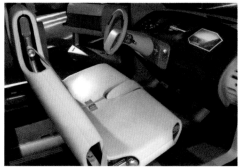

Top: Just as you'd expect of a car unveiled in the year 2000, the 24.7 was intended to represent a look further into the third millennium.

Middle: The cabin design was very open, thanks to the lack of a B-pillar, along with seats that looked almost as though they were floating.

Bottom: The cabin was also stuffed full of neat details, such as the semicircular rearview mirror that incorporated a microphone for the voice-activation of various functions.

Design

Although there were three versions of the 24.7, each featuring a different body style, they all followed the same stylistic themes. Seeming almost as if a product of Fisher-Price, the 24.7's minimalist, angular design appeared incredibly simple at first glance—but the more you looked, the more complex it became.

For example, you'd search in vain for door-mounted mirrors, because they'd been replaced by what Ford called lipstick cameras—presumably because they looked like lipstick tubes on the side of the car, not because they could also apply makeup. These helped boost the 24.7's aerodynamics while also giving the driver a panoramic view of the car's surroundings, projected onto the surface of the instrument panel.

The front doors featured large, square-shape push-button handles that looked more like discreet lighting; once the front doors had been opened, the rear doors (where fitted) could be opened, too, because they were rear-hinged.

The funky styling continued inside, with benchlike seats that were meant to resemble a clamshell. The exterior seat surfaces were covered in a light beige leather, while the inner parts of the shell were painted with the bright yellow accent color seen throughout the interior. Exposed parts of the seat structure were finished in aluminum.

Being the practical one of the bunch, the five-door wagon featured rear seats that folded down flush to the floor to increase the carrying capacity. More neatly, once the vehicle had been powered up and the driver selected, the gauges appeared on the instrument panel in the ideal configuration for that driver. To finish things off, all three 24.7s sat on 17-inch (432-millimeter), six-spoke matte aluminum-finished alloy wheels wrapped in specially cut 245/50R-17 Goodyear tires with what Ford termed "digital patterned tread."

At a Glance

Country of Manufacture
USA

Engine
Front-mounted, normally aspirated four-cylinder gas

Displacement	121 ci (1,988 cc)
Power	111 bhp
Torque	125 lb.-ft.

Drivetrain
Four-speed automatic transmission, front-wheel drive

Suspension, Wheels, and Brakes
Front wheels: 17-in. (432-mm), six-spoke alloy

Rear wheels: 17-in. (432-mm), six-spoke alloy

Front tires: 245/50 R17, made by Goodyear

Rear tires: 245/50 R17, made by Goodyear

Weights and Measurements

Wheelbase	102 in. (2,580 mm)
Length	178 in. (4,530 mm)
Height	57 in. (1,450 mm)

Debut:	Detroit 2000
Design director:	J. Mays

GM Hy-Wire (2003)

There's nothing like ambition for moving things forward—after all, why think small when you can think big? That's clearly what General Motors figured when it set out to "reinvent the car" with its Hy-Wire concept. While marketing hype is expected when it comes to farsighted concepts, in GM's case it was all completely justified; the Hy-Wire really represented Car V2.0.

It may seem somewhat obscure initially, but there's a big clue in the name of the GM Hy-Wire pointing to the technologies that it showcased and why it was so significant, namely hydrogen fuel cell power and drive-by-wire electronics. With two of the most important technologies to enter the automotive field at the start of the twenty-first century, the Hy-Wire was GM's attempt at showing that these techologies could be used in a practical, usable family car— even if there was no chance of the concept making it into production any time soon after it made its debut at the 2003 Detroit Motor Show.

However, GM claimed that a production-ready car that used the Hy-Wire's technologies could be offered by 2010. What GM didn't know, of course, was that a global financial meltdown would strike before then, leading to its own bankruptcy.

The Hy-Wire was a development of the Autonomy concept that General Motors had shown a year earlier—the latter concept showcased the technology, while the former showed how it could all be packaged into a car that could actually be used from day to day. And to really drive the point home, the Hy-Wire was no nonrunning show special—it could be driven just like any production car.

Above: The Hy-Wire looked futuristic, but it still didn't shout about the technology it contained; this really was The Car v2.0.

Left to right: As with so many contemporary concepts, there were rear-hinged back doors for the Hy-Wire, while those lower glass panels were there to emphasize the lack of mechanical linkages prevalent on conventional cars.

Technology

The reason for the importance of the Hy-Wire was its hydrogen fuel cell, the way forward for road cars when the concept was unveiled. Gasoline and diesel engines were highly developed, but they polluted more than the fuel cell and hydrogen was also one of the earth's most abundant elements; fossil fuels were finite resources that were dwindling. The hydrogen-powered fuel-cell stack, which was effectively the Hy-Wire's engine, supplied electricity for the three-phase electric motor. Running continuously, it generated 94 kilowatts (126 brake horsepower) but was capable of peaking at 129 kilowatts (173 brake horsepower).

With the Hy-Wire, the driver had the option of braking and accelerating with either their right or left hand. The driver accelerated by gently twisting either the right or left handgrip, and braked by squeezing the brake actuator also located on the handgrips. The handgrips glided up and down for steering, something that was very different from conventional vehicles where the steering wheel revolved around a steering column.

The drive-by-wire technology was just as important as the use of a fuel cell—if everything continued to be controlled by levers, pulleys, and other mechanical actuators, no real progress could be made in terms of packaging, reductions in production costs, or (to a degree) increasing safety. By introducing solenoids and cables to take care of activating controls for the brakes, clutch, steering, and engine speed, there were all kinds of benefits to be realized, such as clearer, safer, more open cabins.

Top: By removing all the mechanical linkages usually found in a car, the Hy-Wire's cabin could be opened right up.

Middle: Thanks to all those drive-by-wire systems, the Hy-Wire could be switched from left- to right-hand drive in just a few seconds.

Bottom: The Hy-Wire's platform chassis contained all of the propulsion systems, which raised the cabin floor height, but it was also much more open.

Design

The key to the Hy-Wire's potentially low production costs was the "skateboard" construction of the main platform on which the concept was based. This was an 11-inch-thick (279-mm) chassis that housed everything that was needed to make it go, stop, and steer. The initial concept was fitted with a single motor that was located between the front wheels—the aim was for smaller motors to be fitted to each wheel to distribute the power. Between the rear wheels was the fuel-cell stack, while the center of the car housed three hydrogen tanks. The body shell was bolted to all this, which meant it wouldn't be a problem offering several different body styles for any given model range.

By removing the conventional pedal box, there would be more foot-well space and in a collision there would consequently be less hardware in the cabin to cause injuries. The Hy-Wire could also be converted from left-hand drive to right-hand drive in just ten seconds, with the steering wheel moving electrically. Drive-by-wire also allowed for easy tuning of components so that the level of output could be tailored to an individual driver's requirements.

Inside the Hy-Wire there was space for five occupants with room left over for luggage, and to emphasize just how uncluttered the cabin was, plenty of glass was used in the construction. By using glazed units for the front and rear panels, it was possible to see right through the car, while the lack of a B-pillar allowed it to be even more open. Even the backs of the seats featured windowlike recesses, and because there was no engine in front, there was no need for a grille. Consequently, the front of the Hy-Wire was also fitted with a glass panel, so the driver could literally see the road ahead.

The Hy-Wire's "skateboard" chassis held all of the car's essential mechanics, uncluttering the cabin and allowing for interchangeable body styles.

At a Glance

Country of Manufacture
USA/Italy

Engine
Rear-mounted fuel cell of 200 cells connected in series, running 125–200 volts

Fuel Storage System
Three cylindrical high-pressure tanks made of carbon composite, mounted in the middle of the skateboard chassis; total fuel capacity of 4.4 lb. (2 kg)

Power	126 bhp continuous, 173 bhp peak
Torque	159 lb.-ft.

Drivetrain
Three-phase asynchronous electric motor with voltage of 250–380; integrated electronics with planetary gear; single-speed transmission; front-wheel drive

Suspension, Wheels, and Brakes
Front tires: 20 in. (508 mm) in diameter

Rear tires: 22 in. (559 mm) in diameter

Weights and Measurements

Curb weight	4,189 lb. (1,900 kg)
Wheelbase	123 in. (3,114 mm)
Length	195 in. (4,953 mm)
Width	75 in. (1,905 mm)
Height	63 in. (1,593 mm)

Performance

0–40 mph	4.0 seconds
Top speed	40 mph (64 km/h) restricted
Debut:	Detroit 2002

Holden Efijy (2005)

In the first few years of the twenty-first century, there was a battle between America's Big Three (GM, Ford, and Chrysler) to see who could come up with the most retro concept car. In theory, this shouldn't have worked at all—concepts are meant to look forward, not back, after all. However, if you take a motoring icon and update it to the point where it's futuristic instead of just a rehash, you're in the clear, if you can get away with it, which is easier said than done.

Interestingly, while the Big Three frequently revived icons from the 1960s, Holden went back further and brought out this wild concept inspired by its FJ of the 1950s. However, while the lines were distinctly postwar, the technology under the skin was definitely rooted in the twenty-first century.

Based on a redundant Chevrolet Corvette C5 and with a 645 brake horsepower supercharged V8, the Efijy nearly didn't happen. It was started in 2001 but wasn't finished until 2005 because of cash shortages. When it was finally unveiled at the 2005 Sydney Motor Show, the Efijy took the event by storm, although it looked more like something you'd expect to see at a hot rod or custom car show. Unfortunately, however, the whole point of the Efijy was to celebrate the fiftieth anniversary of the FJ, which first went on sale in 1953. The delay in launching it meant the target was missed by a whole two years. Still, that didn't stop the Efijy from being the star of the show.

Of course, there was never any intention of putting the Efijy—or anything like it—into production, but it showcased the talents of an often-forgotten GM outpost. If you're wondering about the name, it was a play on words. With an effigy defined as a "stylistic representation of someone or something famous," and the FJ being an iconic Australian motor vehicle, Holden simply combined the two to come up with the Efijy. Neat.

Above: Retro may have been in when the Efijy was revealed, but nobody had ever created such a retro-futuristic concept as this one.

Left to right: Everywhere you looked there were the kind of details you'd normally see only on a hot rod—and only a superbly crafted one at that.

Technology

The Efijy may have been more than a nod to a past era, but the technology it packed was right up to the minute. The primary evidence of this was the mechanical configuration, which was centered on a supercharged 6-liter Corvette LS6 engine. Naturally, it was fuel injected and driven by ECUs—technologies that were still far in the future when the original FJ Holden was being built. The power plant was efficient and powerful. In fact, with 645 brake horsepower and 560 lb.-ft. of torque, it was nearly 11 times more powerful than the original FJ.

The V8's power was transmitted to the rear wheels via a four-speed automatic transmission and a limited-slip differential. What was more impressive, however, was the electronically controlled air suspension, which could drop the car to just 1 inch (27 millimeters) off the ground, or raise it to 5½ inches (139 millimeters) for when it was being driven—all done at the push of a button.

The custom-designed exhaust was a stainless steel dual system with billet aluminum exhaust tips, while the wheels were enormous billet aluminum items with fluting intended to echo the FJ's more modest original wheels. The brakes meanwhile were 15-inch (381-millimeter) grooved and ventilated discs front and rear, combined with six-piston aluminum calipers at the front and four-piston aluminum calipers at the rear.

The Efijy featured plenty more electronics, too, most notably a major sound system that packed no less than 3,000 watts, including a one-kilowatt amplifier for the subwoofers. The Efijy's entertainment system was definitely something that the designers of the original FJ could only have dreamed about.

Top: The retro theme continued inside, with a dash that could almost have come out of the 1950s—except it was stuffed with all the latest tech.

Middle: The modern tech included a touch-screen multimedia system, which also provided an interface for the climate control.

Bottom: The Efijy was very fast, thanks to its 6-liter supercharged V8, which could generate 645 bhp.

Opposite: The Efijy expertly combined modern technology with retro flair.

Design

The basic exterior design may have been straight from the 1950s, but there were various twenty-first century twists applied. The key one was the lighting, which used LED technology throughout. Brighter and more compact, this LED lighting gave the Efijy a menacing look as well as a high-tech one.

This theme continued inside, where there were plenty of traditional materials, such as wood and leather, but also modern touch-screen controls and digital instrumentation. Yet despite the modern tech, the interior didn't look like a gadget-lover's dream because it was integrated very discreetly into what was fundamentally a 1950s design.

If the detailing looked great, the overall design—inside and out—was nothing less than jaw dropping. The Corvette that provided a basis for the Efijy had to have its chassis lengthened, to the point where the concept was 27½ inches (700 millimeters) longer than the original FJ production car. This gave the concept a much sleeker look, especially when combined with a lowered roofline.

In true hot-rod fashion, the Efijy's exterior lines were uncluttered by extraneous brightwork, although there was some trim, such as the window surrounds and grille. One of the coolest touches was the absence of any door handles; a proximity sensor could tell when the owner was approaching. This would activate a solenoid, popping open the door—once again, the kind of technology that seemed from another galaxy in 1953.

At a Glance

Country of Manufacture
Australia

Engine
Front-mounted, supercharged gas V8

Displacement	6 liters
Power	645 bhp
Torque	560 lb.-ft.

Drivetrain
Four-speed push-button automatic transmission, rear-wheel drive

Suspension, Wheels, and Brakes
Modified from the Chevrolet Corvette

Forged upper and lower control arms featuring height-adjustable air-bag units with electronic control

Front wheels and tires: 20 x 9-in. (508 x 229-mm) alloy wheels with Dunlop SP Sport 9000 255/35 ZR 20 tires
Rear wheels and tires: 22 x 10-in. (559 x 254-mm) alloy wheels with Dunlop SP Sport 9000 285/30 ZR 22 tires
Front brakes: 15-in. (381-mm) grooved and ventilated discs; six-piston aluminum calipers
Rear breaks: 15-in. (381-mm) grooved and ventilated discs; four-piston aluminum calipers

Weights and Measurements

Wheelbase	116 in. (2,946 mm)
Length	203 in. (5,162 mm)
Width	79 in. (1,999 mm)
Height	55 in. (1,386 mm)

Debut:	Sydney 2005
Design director:	Richard Ferlazzo

Hummer HX (2008)

Little did Hummer know that when its HX concept was unveiled early in 2008, the company was set to become one of the biggest automotive hot potatoes in history. So much so that the company was eventually closed down by parent company GM, because Hummer had become an anachronism in little more than two decades after it was founded.

When Hummer arrived on the scene in 1992, it was because its cars were bigger, brasher, and less politically correct than anything that had ever plied U.S. roads so far. The appeal lay in the ridiculous dimensions and profligacy of its cars, but such attributes would remain endearing only for so long, thanks to a group of notoriously fickle buyers.

By 2009, the world had been plunged into recession and the cost of fuel had gone through the roof; even U.S. buyers, renowned for their love of oversized, thirsty cars, decided it was time to tighten their belts. However, before the company disappeared forever, there was just time for one last death-or-glory gasp, and it was the HX concept.

Unveiled at the 2008 Detroit Motor Show, just months before the global financial markets were paralyzed by recession, the HX was meant to hint at a more carefree time when bright young things could fuel up their SUV and head off for the hills to explore.

Keeping in mind the HX's target market, it was designed by three young designers from within GM's own design studios. The thinking was that by choosing twenty-somethings to design the HX, it would be that much more appealing to such a target audience. When the HX was unveiled, the company gushed: "The HX is Hummer's vision: an agile, trail-ready, open-air vehicle that fits the lifestyles of everyone who needs or wants to drive off-road. Of course, it carries exceptional off-road capability and the distinctive styling for which all Hummers are known." Unfortunately, it wasn't to be.

Above: The HX was too little, too late; when it was revealed, the company was about to enter its death throes before being wound up.

Left to right: Although Hummer had never built anything like the HX before—at least not for production—there was no mistaking it was the company behind this concept, thanks to a raft of classic design cues.

Technology

While everyone else was embracing electric drive and hybrid technology, Hummer remained resolutely wedded to gasoline power for the HX. However, there were signs of the company becoming a little bit more ecologically aware, because the HX power plant displaced just 3.6 liters and featured a V6 configuration; a couple of years earlier there would no doubt have been a V8 in the front end that displaced at least 5.7 liters. Also, the HX's V6 didn't have to be fed only a diet of unleaded gasoline; it was engineered to run on 85 percent biofuel to help reduce CO_2 emissions.

A full-time 4WD system pulled the HX over, through, and around off-road obstacles. It transferred torque to the front and rear axles, each of which was equipped with a locking differential. The tires were custom-made 35-inch-tall (885-millimeter) off-road items mounted on bead-lock-style wheels. The front suspension featured an electronic-disconnecting stabilizer bar for enhanced maneuverability when driving off-road, with things helped further by its heavy-duty shock absorbers.

Other than that, the Hummer was pretty low-tech; this concept was all about appealing to a new demographic rather than trying to dazzle with new innovations. As such, the HX was engineered to cope with inhospitable terrain, whether that was rocks, water up to 2 feet (609 mm) deep, or shifting sands. If you were heading out into the wilds, the Hummer HX was intended to do a better job than anything else available.

Top: Black, orange, and silver doesn't sound like a great set of colors for a car interior—not even for a concept—but the HX's cabin looked great.

Middle: All that alloy was supposed to make the HX's cabin look as though it had been taken from an aircraft; it certainly looked high-tech.

Bottom: Somehow a Hummer didn't seem right without a V8 up front, but the HX packed just six cylinders—but there was still over 300 bhp on tap.

Design

The HX was intended to showcase a Hummer that would be smaller, lighter, and nimbler than anything that had previously been seen from the company. It would still have all those aggressive styling cues of the much bigger, military-inspired Hummers, but the HX would be a little less intimidating, although not *that* much less.

Unlike previous Hummers, the HX featured just two doors—an indication of its relatively sporty intent. For added fun, there were two removable roof panels, as well as a tailgate and rear side panels that could be removed. Hummer claimed the HX was a convertible, but it wasn't really, because the bodywork configuration wasn't all that flexible. Besides, with everything removed, there was nowhere in the car to store these pieces.

If you got carried away while your socket set was out, you could also remove the wheel-arch extensions that were fitted at each corner, turning the HX into an open-wheeler. The doors could also be removed, thanks to specially built hinges; all of this was to appease serious off-road enthusiasts who like their cars to be as open as possible when tackling the rough stuff.

So while the HX was like no Hummer ever built in series, it still featured all those classic design cues that made it instantly recognizable as an offshoot of the infamous GM brand. The circular headlights in round housings, upright windshield, minimal overhangs, plus assorted vents and air intakes, were all classic Hummer. Not that any of this did the company any good; its days were numbered even before the HX had been designed, never mind built.

Intended to give an air of lightness and strength, the HX's cabin was a mixture of matte-finished olive and aluminum alloy with four individual bucket seats instead of the more usual bench seat; those in the rear could be removed to create more carrying space. With a rubberized floor and synthetic coverings on the dash, this wasn't the place to find luxury.

At a Glance

Country of Manufacture
USA

Engine
Front-mounted, normally aspirated gas V6

Displacement	217 ci (3,564 cc)
Power	304 bhp
Torque	273 lb.-ft.

Drivetrain
Six-speed automatic transmission, full-time four-wheel drive with front and rear locking differentials

Suspension, Wheels, and Brakes
Front: Independent SLA, custom coil-over shocks; 2-in. (51-mm) shocks, 2.5-in. (63.5-mm) springs

Rear: Semitrailing link, custom coil-over shocks; 2-in. (51-mm) shocks, 2.5-in. (63.5-mm) springs

15-in. (381-mm) discs all around with six-piston calipers at the front and four-piston calipers at the rear

20 x 9-in. (508 x 229-mm) alloy wheels front and rear with 35-in. (889-m) Bridgestone Dueler tires

Weights and Measurements

Wheelbase	103 in. (2,616 mm)
Length	171 in. (4,343 mm)
Width	81 in. (2,057 mm)
Height	72 in. (1,829 mm)
Debut:	Detroit 2008

Infiniti Essence (2009)

Although Infiniti had launched in the United States in 1989, it would be another two decades before the Nissan subsidiary would make it to Europe, by which time arch rival Lexus was already well established. However, it wasn't this Toyota subbrand that was Infiniti's greatest threat—it was the German trio of Audi, BMW, and Mercedes that would give it the hardest time. So when Infiniti finally appeared in Europe in 2009, it had to put on a pretty good show if it wasn't to be dismissed out of hand. And what an introduction the Essence made.

Unsurprisingly, Infiniti focused on great engineering and excellent reliability to sell its cars, but for such a notoriously conservative market segment, its cars were also pretty eye-catching. The thing was, in Europe when the Essence was launched, the Infiniti brand was largely unknown and so was the company's design language. As a result, despite 20 years of history, Infiniti was in a situation where it could effectively work with a blank sheet of paper to reinvent itself.

With Infiniti's production cars more distinctive than most in the segment, the Essence had to really push the boundaries, which is exactly what it did. There wasn't a straight edge in sight, and while the curvacious bodywork was somewhat complex when you analyzed it, everything was coherent. More important was that while at first glance the Essence looked every inch the concept, it didn't look as though it was completely unattainable—it was the kind of thing that Infiniti could realistically have put into production without having to water down the exterior design too much.

Above: The Infiniti Essence packed cutting-edge technology while also looking utterly beautiful and aggressive at the same time.

Left to right: The polished finish for the panelwork set off the Essence's curves beautifully—whichever angle you viewed it from, there wasn't a straight line in sight.

Technology

Lexus had made a name for itself as the only manufacturer of premium hybrids, and many more carmakers were set to jump on the gasoline/electric bandwagon, including companies such as Audi and Porsche. So it made sense for Infiniti to play the eco card, too, by creating a concept that packed the latest technology and looked sensational: the Essence scored heavily on both counts.

At the heart of the Essence was a 434 brake horsepower 3.7-liter V6 gasoline engine that was mated with an electric motor that could produce another 158 brake horsepower. However, while the engine was pretty conventional, aside from a direct-injection fuel system, the motor was cutting edge. Called a 3D motor, it was much more compact than a conventional unit, while also being twice as torquey. Power for the motor came from a set of lithium-ion batteries that were charged by the engine; a regenerative braking system also helped to top them up.

The other key technologies touted by the Essence were all based on safety and wore Safety Shield branding. This was comprised of adaptive cruise control and lane departure warning, adding side collision prevention and rear collision prevention. The latter worked by sensing a vehicle in front of the Essence when it was in motion and giving the driver a warning—and if this wasn't heeded, the brakes would be activated automatically. The idea with all this technology was that the Essence was protected from every direction, thus making it virtually impossible to crash. Well, that was the theory, anyway.

Top: For a concept car, the Essence featured a surprisingly understated interior. However, it was none the worse for it, thanks to the tasteful brown-and-black color theme.

Middle: In typical Japanese fashion, Infiniti couldn't resist spicing up the dash display a little, so it looked like something from an arcade game.

Bottom: Everywhere you looked in the cabin of the Essence there were beautiful design details and premium materials.

Opposite: The roof of the car was made entirely of glass, which brightened the cabin.

Design

Infiniti produced even more marketing hype for the Essence than usual. There were reams of text about brand values, intellectual heroes, and passion, but it all distilled down to a straightforward approach. Essence buyers would be inspired by the car's understated good looks, which would set trends instead of follow them. As a result, the Essence wasn't flash or contrived, but was eye-catching from every angle and up to the minute with its detailing, which worked superbly. Indeed, Infiniti summed it up pretty well in the accompanying blurb: "It looks like a driver's car, one that would be right at home spearing down the world's grandest motoring routes."

The Essence wasn't just an opportunity for Infiniti's suits to go into hyperdrive with their marketing puff; it was intended to signal a new design direction for the company—one that would offer huge presence while still looking discreet and quality instead of quantity.

With its short rear deck and long, flowing hood, the Essence looked every inch the grand tourer. The accentuated wheel arches front and rear lent an air of muscularity. The rear section also featured complex surfacing with concave scoops that flowed down the rear-pillars from one of the Essence's most distinctive design cues: a C-shape kink to the side windows' trailing edge. Outlined by a wide flourish of stainless steel, it gave the Essence an even more dynamic look—not that it really needed it.

At a Glance

Country of Manufacture
Japan/USA

Engine
Front-mounted, normally aspirated gas V6, plus rear-mounted lithium-ion battery

Displacement	3.7 liters
Power	434 bhp (engine) + 158 bhp (electric motor)
Torque	369 lb.-ft.

Drivetrain
Six-speed semiautomatic transmission, rear-wheel drive

Suspension, Wheels, and Brakes
22-in. (559-mm) wheels front and rear

Weights and Measurements

Wheelbase	110 in. (2,800 mm)
Length	186 in. (4,720 mm)
Width	77 in. (1,960 mm)
Height	52 in. (1,310 mm)

Performance

Fuel economy	35 mpg approx.
CO_2 emissions	190 g/km
Debut:	Geneva 2009

Jaguar F-Type (2000)

When it comes to seminal sports cars, there can be none more iconic than the Jaguar E-Type, first seen in 1961 and now one of the world's most recognizable automotive shapes. But where do you go from there? Do you try to cash in on such a revered car or do you try to move on by barely acknowledging it? If you're in any doubt, just looking at the F-Type's name will provide the answer—although the concept owed more to the XK8 that was then in production rather than the E-Type that had bowed out a quarter of a century before. The F-Type made its debut at the 2000 Geneva Motor Show.

Whereas the XK8, and Jaguars in general, had become portly thanks to somewhat generous dimensions, the F-Type intended to reverse the trend. The F-Type had started out as a project overseen by Jaguar's then head of design Geoff Lawson. However, when Lawson died suddenly in June 1999, Keith Helfet became the design project leader, and the result of his team's efforts was one of the most beautiful and curvaceous concepts ever seen.

In the end, the F-Type's chances of making it into production were scuttled by the need for a custom-made platform if it was to retain its compact dimensions. Engineering a floor plan just for the one model proved to be prohibitively expensive, and there was no way Jaguar would have got its money back from such a move. By basing the car on an existing platform, it would have become a different car—and when Porsche tried to do that with its 911-based Boxster, it lost something between the concept and production stages. Jaguar didn't want to fall into that trap, even if the Boxster did prove greatly profitable for Porsche.

Ultimately, all was not lost. While talk of a Jaguar F-Type regularly cropped up in motoring magazines—the title effectively being shorthand for a modern-day compact sports car—there were no production cars unveiled. However, at the 2011 Frankfurt Motor Show, Jaguar unveiled its C-X16 concept: a thinly veiled early view of a production car that was intended to sit in much the same market segment as the F-Type.

Above: For decades, Jaguar traded on its heritage—specifically the fabulous E-Type. The F-Type suggested something sexy was once more on the way.

Left to right: The F-Type was unmistakably Jaguar, with all those compound curves and the faired-in headlights. However, the company had never offered a barchetta like this before.

Technology

Jaguar released few details of the technology that the F-Type packed, largely because it didn't actually pack that much. With the concept being little more than a rolling shell, all that Jaguar really had to say on the topic was that the headlights "employed an adaptation of the latest Baroptic light guide technology in a unique multiple-element cluster." If that means anything to you, you're doing well—but suffice it to say that the headlights should have been brighter than was usual for the time.

There was no engine or running gear for the show car, but it was envisioned that a 2.5- or 3.0-liter V6, as seen in the X-Type, would fit the bill. In standard form, it would produce in the order of 240 brake horsepower, but with the aid of a supercharger, a very healthy 300 brake horsepower could easily be realized.

Of course, there was always the option of installing the V8 already seen in the very desirable XK8 coupé and convertible, but by doing so the F-Type would have encroached on the territory of its more upscale sibling, which came with only that power plant, in normally aspirated or supercharged forms. What Jaguar definitely wouldn't have done is fit a diesel engine or anything high-tech incorporating hybrid technology; at this stage in the company's development, it was definitely a case of getting the cars to sell largely on their looks.

In terms of transmissions, manual or automatic transmissions would be available with rear-wheel drive being standard—although four-wheel drive would probably have been an option on the more powerful models.

Top: Although the F-Type's dash looked complicated, this was actually a back-to-basics sports car with old-fashioned analog instrumentation.

Middle: Most of the switch gear within the cabin was handmade specially for this concept from alloy.

Bottom: The F-Type was a compact sports car designed to take on the Audi TT and Mercedes SLK— but it was far more beautiful.

Opposite: This photo shows just how much the F-Type owed to the E-Type.

Design

The reasoning behind the F-Type was that it could provide a British competitor to the Porsche Boxster, Mercedes SLK, BMW Z3, and Audi TT Roadster—a market then worth 150,000 cars annually. Although any production model would have to be eminently practical, the show car didn't need to worry about such boring details, which is why there was no weather protection of any kind.

Although the F-Type would be a sports car capable of high speeds, there were no skirts, spoilers, or other aerodynamic distractions on the bodywork. Whether or not the car would have proved stable at high speed with such smooth lines isn't known, but the diffuser at the back of the car, combined with a smooth underbody, should have done their bit to maintain stability as the speed built. At the front there was a very subtle adjustable air dam, which could be lowered automatically at high speed to reduce lift. However, despite the best efforts of the design team, there would still have been major problems with turbulence over the car's occupants as speeds rose because of the total absence of any kind of roof.

Inside the F-Type there was a simple but high-tech approach. Aluminum abounded, with much of it machined from solid and then polished to perfection. Virtually all of the switch gear was made from solid pieces of alloy to give a beautifully engineered, tactile quality.

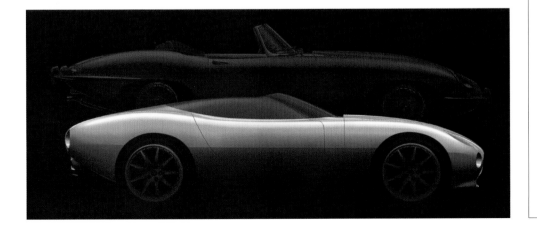

At a Glance

Country of Manufacture
UK

Engine
Front-mounted, gas V6; the concept was a nonrunner, but the S-Type's 3-liter V6 was proposed

Displacement	181 ci (2,967 cc)
Power	240 bhp
Torque	221 lb.-ft.

Drivetrain
Five-speed semiautomatic transmission, rear-wheel drive

Suspension, Wheels, and Brakes
Ventilated disc brakes front and rear

Weights and Measurements

Wheelbase	94 in. (2,400 mm)
Length	162 in. (4,115 mm)
Width	68 in. (1,732 mm)
Height	43 in. (1,090 mm)

Debut:	Detroit 2000
Exterior designer:	Keith Helfet
Interior designers:	Adam Hatton
	Pasi Pennanen
Design directors:	Ian Callum
	Geoff Lawson

Jeep Hurricane (2005)

The Chrysler Group has been no stranger to extreme concept cars over the years, but its Jeep division has typically been less forthcoming when it comes to shock-and-awe tactics. However, after a string of completely insane concepts from the Chrysler Group, such as the Dodge Tomahawk and Chrysler ME412, it was Jeep's turn in 2005 with a concept that was pretty much as far removed from reality as it's possible to get.

Bizarrely, the premise for the Hurricane was "responsible excess"—somebody within Jeep decided that they wanted to test the theory that such a thing could exist. There was no doubt that the Hurricane represented excess in abundance, but it was hard, if not impossible, to see where the responsibility part came in. After all, any car with two 5.7-liter V8 engines that between them produced nearly 700 brake horsepower and over 700 lb.-ft. of torque could only ever be perceived as somewhat over the top.

When it was unveiled, the Hurricane was billed as "the most maneuverable, most capable, and most powerful 4x4 ever built"—a claim with which it was hard to disagree. After all, with both axles capable of turning, the Hurricane was capable of spinning within its own axis.

While such a facility may seem like the ultimate in pointlessness, Jeep justified it by saying that: "Out in the wilderness, changing direction in minimal space can mean the difference between an afternoon of adventure and a distress call back to the trailhead. The multimode four-wheel steering system is designed to offer enthusiasts the next level of performance and unexpected maneuverability."

However, despite such functionality supposedly being indispensable to those intent on hardcore off-roading, so far none of the technologies showcased by the Hurricane have made production anywhere, and it's not hard to see why.

Above: There was no mistaking which carmaker was responsible for the Hurricane, thanks to those open fenders and that classic seven-bar grille.

Left to right: With its raised ride height, the Hurricane was capable of going pretty much anywhere, but the craziest thing of all was the steering; the car could turn in its length, virtually.

Technology

Although the Hurricane was meant to be the most powerful and capable Jeep ever, it could also be surprisingly green thanks to its multidisplacement engine. It could run on 4, 8, 12, or 16 cylinders, depending on power requirements—and the distance of the car from the nearest fuel stop. When accelerating as quickly as possible, all 16 cylinders from both V8s would be burning fuel at the fastest possible rate to develop the full 670 horses. In this mode, the Hurricane was capable of despatching the 0-to-60 sprint in under five seconds—the kind of figures usually associated with something a lot lower and a lot sleeker.

As with any Jeep, go-anywhere ability was the Hurricane's forté, the key to which was massive axle articulation. Naturally, there was independent suspension all around; a double-wishbone setup that provided a serious 20 inches (508 millimeters) of travel. Of course, there was also full-time four-wheel drive; the power was delivered through a central transfer case and split axles with a mechanically controlled four-wheel torque distribution system.

For added manueverability, the Hurricane featured two modes of automated four-wheel steering. The first was conventional, with the rear tires turning in the opposite direction from the front to reduce the turning circle. The second mode was targeted at off-road drivers: all four wheels turned in the same direction for nimble crab steering, allowing for the car to move sideways without changing the direction it was pointing.

Top: The rear-wheel steering wasn't the only crazy design feature; the fact that the Hurricane packed a V8 at each end was also off its rocker.

Middle: By allowing all four wheels to turn, the Hurricane could be manoeuvred in even the tightest spot, on or off the road.

Bottom: Although efficiency wasn't especially important, the Hurricane featured a lot of carbon fiber in a bid to keep its weight down.

Opposite: From the top, the Hurricane almost looks like a normal Jeep.

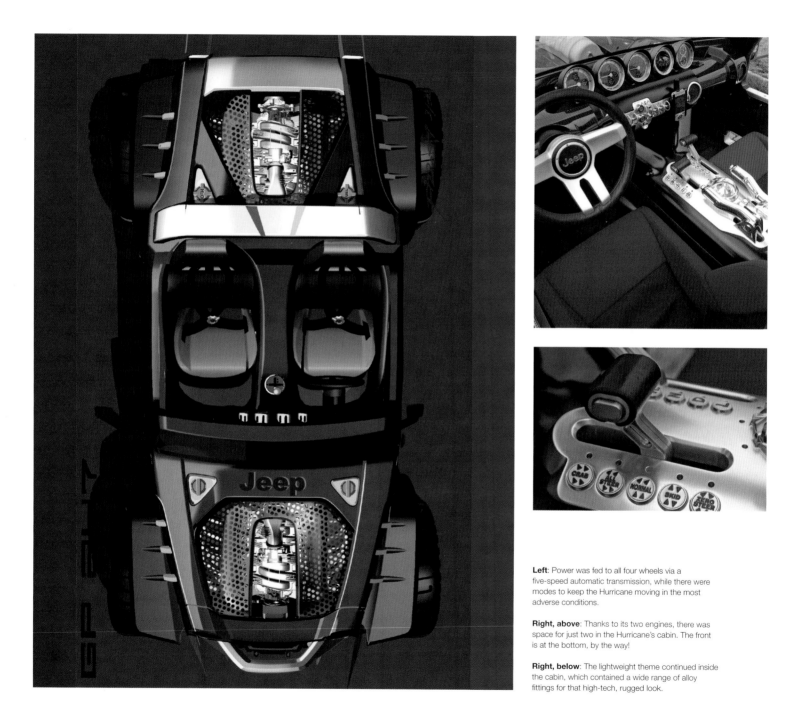

Left: Power was fed to all four wheels via a five-speed automatic transmission, while there were modes to keep the Hurricane moving in the most adverse conditions.

Right, above: Thanks to its two engines, there was space for just two in the Hurricane's cabin. The front is at the bottom, by the way!

Right, below: The lightweight theme continued inside the cabin, which contained a wide range of alloy fittings for that high-tech, rugged look.

Design

You didn't have to study the Hurricane very closely to work out who made it; this could only ever be a product of the fertile imaginations of Jeep's designers. Those hugely flared wheel arches, the massive ground clearance, and that iconic seven-bar grille all gave the game away, along with the circular headlights and heavily tapered hood.

What Jeep hadn't done before, however, was to build a car with an engine in the front and another in the back for good measure. That meant practicality had to take a back seat—well, if the Hurricane had been fitted with one, that may have been the case. There was space strictly for two, with each occupant getting a snug cloth-trimmed bucket seat.

The interior was something of a masterpiece, because it looked rather luxurious at first glance but was actually pretty functional. Featuring a lot of brushed aluminum, the most high-tech aspect of its appearance was the GPS system, which was clipped to the dash.

Intriguingly, the one-piece unibody was shaped of carbon fiber; this unitary design meant the body shell incorporated the separate chassis that would normally be used on this type of car. It also allowed the suspension and power train to be mounted directly to the body, while there was an aluminum spine, which ran under the body to strengthen the underside and also to function as a complete skid-plate system.

To complete the rugged look, there were alloy wheels, which measured a hefty 20 inches (508 millimeters) in diameter; also 10 inches (254 millimeters) wide, they were wrapped in 305/70 R20 tires. It was these tires, along with the minimal overhangs, that gave the Hurricane its tremendous maneuverability; with approach and departure angles of 64 and 86.7 degrees, respectively, you'd have to search hard to find any terrain that would beat this Jeep.

At a Glance

Country of Manufacture
USA

Engine
Front- and rear-mounted, normally aspirated gas V8s

Displacement	345 ci (5,654 cc) x 2
Power	3,35 bhp x 2 (670 bhp)
Torque	370 lb.-ft. x 2 (740 lb.-ft.)

Drivetrain
Five-speed automatic transmission, four-wheel drive

Suspension, Wheels, and Brakes
Front suspension: Double wishbone with coil springs

Rear suspension: Double wishbone with coil springs

Wheels: 20 x 10-in. (508 x 254-mm) alloy wheels front and rear

Tires: 305/70 R20 front and rear

Weights and Measurements

Curb weight	3,849 lb. (1,746 kg)
Wheelbase	108 in. (2,746 mm)
Length	152 in. (3,856 mm)
Width	80 in. (2,033 mm)
Height	68 in. (1,732 mm)

Performance

0–62 mph	Less than 5 seconds
Debut:	Detroit 2005

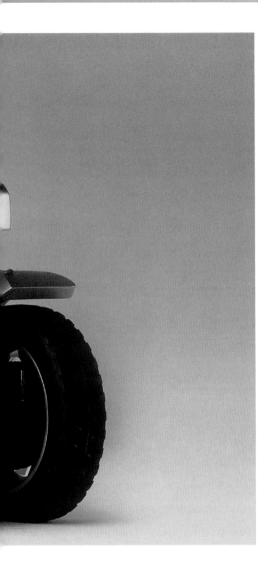

Jeep Treo (2003)

If you had to come up with the most profligate cars ever built, your list would no doubt consist of a list of SUVs, including—most likely—a string of products from Jeep. However, if the Treo had gone into production, there's no way it would have belonged on such a list because this would have been the most efficient and compact car ever to wear a Jeep badge. Indeed, it would have been one of the most compact and efficient cars of any kind.

Jeep summed it up pretty well in its introductory press release, which stated that the Treo offered, "A vivid new interpretation of where the Jeep brand could go in the future. The Jeep Treo exemplifies the idea of 'fluid imagination' thinking in a stunning, unexpected package—a form and presence that challenges the brand's traditional dimensions, but in the end, can still be viewed as authentically Jeep. The Treo is the next-generation, urban-active Jeep—one that will allow it to thrive in a city or campus environment, yet one that will easily take its owner to the trailhead. All of this adaptable with the ability to use the freedom of fuel-cell technology."

If you're wondering just how small the Treo was, there's a clue in the name, because it could seat only three people. Keeping in mind most Jeeps can comfortably accommodate more or less double this, the Treo was a departure for a company that until now had always assumed that the maxim "biggest means best" contained more than a mere grain of truth.

The purpose of the Treo was to offer stylish urban transport for young drivers who also wanted to escape the city on the weekends and enjoy some outdoor pursuits. As a result, there was ample ground clearance and most of the other characteristics you'd expect of a Jeep—just in a smaller package. So there were large wheels with ultragrippy tires along with exposed towing eyes front and rear. Nevertheless, Jeep never had the courage to build the Treo—or anything like it—in any form. Even a conventionally powered Treo would have been a breath of fresh air, but its compact dimensions meant there just wouldn't have been the space to accommodate the necessary engine and transmission. Maybe one day . . .

Above: There really was nothing like the Treo, which featured open wheels and seating for just three. Frankly, it didn't make any sense.

Left to right: Jeep had never made anything as compact as this; it flew in the face of everything the company stood for in that it was small and efficient, not a brute of an off-roader.

Technology

The Treo was a nonrunner because the technology it was envisioned to adopt was definitely from several years—or even decades—in the future. Motive power would come from a hydrogen fuel cell, which would power a pair of electric motors. There would be permanent four-wheel drive, but not at the expense of efficiency; this would be a car that would also be among the cleanest on the planet with ultralow CO_2 emissions.

Because the Treo didn't run, it didn't have to feature a working fuel-cell or viable fuel-storage system, so Jeep's designers didn't have to consider real-world packaging requirements all that much. Whether or not a fuel tank and cell could have been accommodated within the Treo's compact confines is open to debate, but one thing that would have made things a lot easier was a move to drive-by-wire.

By dispensing with the usual linkages, pipes, shafts, and levers that control the brakes, steering, and other drive systems of a car, Jeep used electrics and electronics instead for a full drive-by-wire system. As a result, the limited amount of space available could be used much more efficiently, while the cabin could also be opened up more.

By adopting drive-by-wire, the Treo was automatically also safer, but there was also another major benefit—not for the user, but for Jeep itself. It could slash manufacturing costs by not having to engineer Treos for different markets depending on whether they were left- or right-hand drive, because the car could be switched from one to the other with a minimum of effort.

Top: The Treo was very much a lifestyle vehicle, which is why Jeep made provision for a pair of bikes to be carried on its back.

Middle: To improve fuel efficiency, the Treo sat on narrow tires, but they featured a decently wide track in an effort to improve stability.

Bottom: The interior couldn't have been much simpler; there was effectively a bench seat and the minimum of controls or instrumentation.

Design

If you'd removed the Jeep badges from the Treo, you'd probably have struggled to identify it as a Jeep, except for one aspect: that classic seven-bar grille. While even now Jeep builds cars that feature enormous flared wheel arches, the Treo went a stage further with its open-wheeled design. As a result, the passenger cell was surprisingly narrow; with the car having an overall width of just 5 feet 6 inches (1,680 millimeters), the cabin was amazingly compact for something wearing Jeep badges.

While the open-wheeled layout was certainly eye-catching, the most unusual aspect of the Treo's design was its tapered body. Because the rear of the car was so narrow, it was necessary to mount a small fin at the top of each rear quarter panel to house the lighting units; they also acted as anchorage points for a pair of mountain bikes. And while the whole of the Treo's rear could be opened up with a vertically hinged tailgate, there wasn't a lot of carrying capacity in the load bay—so if mountain bikes did need to be carried, the only way of doing so was by leaving them on the outside.

Just like the exterior, the interior didn't look much like anything ever to have come out of a Jeep factory. The very narrow cabin meant Jeep's designers had to be pretty focused to fit everything in; the result was a minimalist interior that featured two seats butted up to each other. In front of these was a dash that was incredibly simple in its layout and features; a single binnacle in front of the driver was the highlight, but there was a neat twist. By mounting the binnacle and steering wheel on a sliding module, the car could be converted from left- to right-hand drive in seconds, helped by the use of drive-by-wire technology throughout.

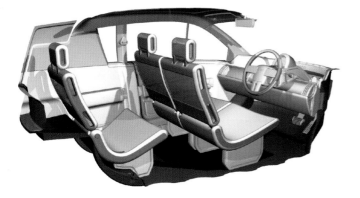

Because the body shell was tapered heavily toward the rear, there was space for just a single seat in the back of the Treo.

At a Glance

Country of Manufacture
USA

Engine
Rear-mounted fuel cell driving one electric motor for each axle

Drivetrain
Six-speed semiautomatic transmission, four-wheel drive

Suspension, Wheels, and Brakes
Wheels: 19 x 6-in. (483 x 152-mm) alloy wheels front and rear

Tires: 185/65 R19 tires front and rear

Weights and Measurements

Curb weight	1,799 lb. (816 kg)
Wheelbase	96 in. (2,450 mm)
Length	127 in. (3,235 mm)
Width	66 in. (1,680 mm)
Height	62 in. (1,585 mm)
Ground clearance	8 in. (200 mm)
Debut:	Tokyo 2003

Karmann Sport Utility Cabriolet (2005)

For some reason, carmakers and coach builders are constantly trying to reinvent the wheel. As if there aren't enough types of cars already available, there's always someone on the lookout for the next big thing. The result has been a multitude of crossover vehicles over the years. While this term has generally come to mean a compact SUV, in reality it's the result of any segments being combined—and in some cases it can be more than just two.

Take the Karmann SUC, for example, otherwise known as the Karmann Sport Utility Cabriolet. Karmann went bust in 2009 and it's not hard to see why, when it was focusing its efforts on projects as crazy as this one. If ever there was a type of car guaranteed to prove impossible to resolve economically, it's the four-door convertible. Throw in the SUV configuration as a starting point and you just know you're doomed to fail. That didn't stop Karmann from dreaming up the SUC, however, in conjunction with transmission specialist ZF. The duo had their work cut out trying to overcome the packaging, rigidity, and safety issues inherent in a car such as this, so there was never any possibility of the car being commercially available.

However, give credit where it's due; Karmann's designers and engineers came up with a fully driveable prototype that worked properly. Its roof raised and stowed, kept out the elements, and sealed properly, although there was little chance of anything like the SUC ever making production. However, despite the SUC being doomed from the outset, it provided a great showcase for Karmann's talents, and because it worked with various large carmakers, there was always the chance of one of them adopting the technology for a luxury convertible—after all, by doing so, they'd be able to distance themselves from rivals.

So, while the SUC made little sense at any level, it was a feat of engineering because it managed to find solutions to complex problems, even if the end result was something that you could hardly call attractive.

Above: With the roof up, you'd have been hard put to tell that the SUC was a convertible, so neat was the design of the folding roof.

Left to right: The rear styling was more of a success than that of the front end, especially with the roof stowed away. However, even with it up, the SUC looked good.

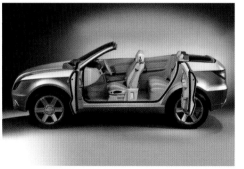

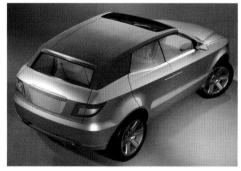

Technology

All of the running gear was taken from the BMW X5, which meant there was a V8 gasoline engine and four-wheel drive. That wasn't a bad starting point because the X5 was reckoned to be the best-handling SUV available at the time, with the possible exception of Porsche's Cayenne.

However, while the X5 provided an impressive base car, it was only ever meant to be a starting point; once partner ZF had got to work on it, the SUC's dynamic capabilities were even more impressive. That's because ZF added a multitude of sensors to create a series of safety systems that allowed the car to seemingly defy the laws of physics while also improving handling and even refinement. Just as crucially, ZF's work also ensured that if the SUC was taken into an off-road situation, its ample power could be deployed to whichever wheel was best able to cope. Keeping in mind the SUC's configuration, it would have been fascinating to see just how stiff its structure proved to be when tackling some really rough terrain.

Ultimately, the SUC's underpinnings weren't really all that important, because it was what they put on top that mattered. That's because the point of the SUC was to pioneer a seriously impressive folding roof mechanism that allowed a much larger roof than usual to fold away out of sight once stowed. Indeed, the folding cloth roof was something of a masterpiece, because it incorporated a polycarbonate sunroof, yet it still folded flush when stowed. This sunroof could be tilted for extra ventilation with the roof up, and even when the car was in closed mode, the roof didn't look ungainly—something that would have been understandable keeping in mind the generous proportions of the SUC. With an area of about 43 square feet (4 meters squared), the SUC's roof was the largest fully automatic cabriolet roof in the world, even if it was a one of a kind.

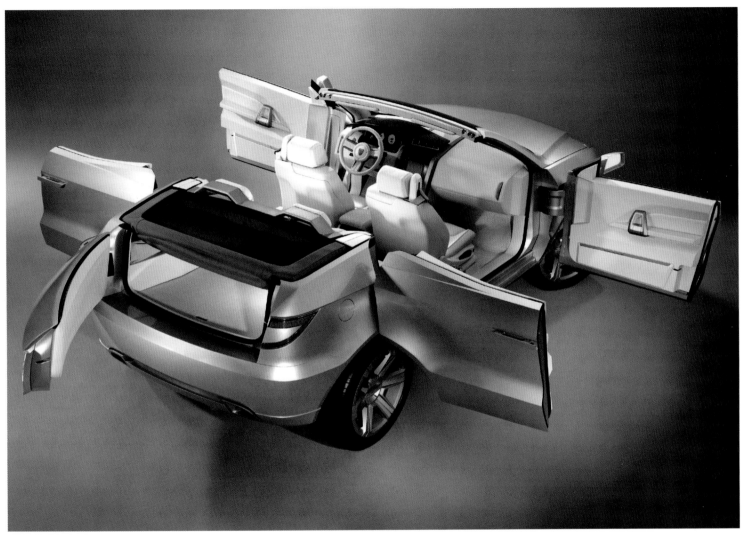

Opposite, top: Intended to be premium, the SUC had large wheels wrapped in low-profile tires.

Opposite, middle: Cream leather meant the SUC's cabin felt light and airy even with the roof up.

Opposite, bottom: It's amazing that the SUC's body shell had any rigidity at all with its four-door pillarless configuration.

Above: The SUC was designed to open up completely for people and cargo.

Left: The SUC didn't look much like a performance car, but there were paddle shifts on the steering wheel for enthusiast driving.

Top: Thanks to the stiff body shell and ample performance from the BMW-sourced V8, the SUC should have been good to drive.

Above: The SUC also pioneered high-tech lighting front and rear, which meant that the tail lights incorporated neatly styled LED clusters.

Opposite: The SUC's front end was particularly ugly, thanks to a combination of design misjudgments.

Design

At first glance the SUC looked like the Renault Koleos—a compact SUV that bombed globally. However, while the Koleos was ugly, the SUC took this lack of attractiveness to new heights— it was as though Karmann's design team had set out to create as ugly a car as possible. While the sculpted sides and overall profile looked pretty good, the front end was a mess with its lack of grille, oversize badge, and vents in an awkward size sitting below the headlights.

While the roof was an impressive feat of engineering, so was the ingenious glass rear window, which retracted electrically into the tailgate when the roof was stowed. Behind the rear seats were a pair of pop-up roll hoops for protection in the event of the car rolling; once again, these were neatly integrated so that they worked whether the roof was up or down.

Karmann didn't make things easy for itself, however, because as if making a four-door convertible rigid wasn't difficult enough, there was no B-pillar at all. As a result, the rear doors opened backward—something that was starting to become fashionable in production sedans, such as the Mazda RX-8 and Rolls-Royce Phantom.

At a Glance

Country of Manufacture
Germany

Engine
Front-mounted gas V8

Displacement	278 ci (4,401 cc)
Power	320 bhp
Torque	324 lb.-ft.

Drivetrain
Six-speed automatic transmission, four-wheel drive

Suspension, Wheels, and Brakes
Front tires:	295/45 R22
Rear tires:	295/45 R22

Weights and Measurements
Wheelbase	111 in. (2,820 mm)
Length	183 in. (4,638 mm)
Width	86 in. (2,180 mm)
Height	69 in. (1,750 mm)

Performance
0–62 mph	8 seconds approx.
Top speed	130 mph (209 km/h) approx.
Debut:	Frankfurt 2005

Kia POP (2010)

Kia hasn't been afraid to unveil a lot of concepts over the years, but most of the company's early attempts left much to be desired stylistically. For a company perceived as at the budget end of the market, Kia needed to prove that it had ideas in terms of design and technology to show that it was going places. However, in the early days, Kia's concepts generally only reinforced the view that it couldn't quite cut it with the big boys.

The appointment of Peter Schreyer in 2006 proved a turning point for the company; by 2007, he'd already made his mark with the unveiling of the Kee concept. Schreyer had worked for Audi prior to Kia; he was best known for his iconic TT sports car, so he'd already shown he could come up with distinctive designs. The Kee, with its new tiger front end, signaled a new look for Kia—one that would filter down to its production models soon after.

What the Kee didn't do was signal the start of a change in direction for Kia. This was a sporting coupé, and Kia didn't really have the image to move into such a niche, even if its cousin Hyundai had been selling coupés for years. However, if the Kee seemed far removed from reality for Kia, the seriously avant garde POP of 2010 went even further.

Everything about the POP was at least unusual, if not futuristic. So while the overall shape and some of the technology it packed were from an era yet to come, the purple interior and chrome exterior just screamed individuality. And while most of Kia's production cars offered a more homogenous design until this point, the arrival of the POP marked the start of some eye-catching models, such as the Sportage and second-generation Picanto. However, unfortunately, nothing like the POP.

Above: Kia's design had come on in leaps and bounds in a very short space of time, but none of its road cars looked as good as this.

Left to right: Kia had never created a two-seater city car before, but you'd never know it; from every angle the POP looked sensational, especially in profile.

Technology

While the POP was created primarily to show the creativity of Kia's European design studios, it was also up to the minute in terms of technology. As a city car, minimalism was the name of the game, so it wasn't packed from bumper to bumper with the latest high-tech gadgetry, but it did feature an ultramodern drivetrain. At the heart of this was purely electric propulsion—a power source that was starting to gain acceptance in production cars, even if that acceptance was pretty limited.

The motor fitted was a 50-kilowatt unit that also offered a useful 140 lb.-ft. of torque—perfect for nipping about town in silence. With a 30-minute fast recharge time and a 100-mile (160-kilometer) range, the POP was more usable than most electric cars, although whether or not the car could be made in electric form at an affordable price was another matter.

The POP's cabin wasn't especially well stocked with gadgets, because things were kept pretty simple. However, there was an interesting piece of tech for the driver; a small piece of plexiglass that displayed all the car's key functions. Known as a TOLED, or Transparent Organic LED, this head-up display was more efficient than the usual design in that it was self-contained and didn't need a separate projector.

Top: The POP's cabin was tiny, so in a bid to make it feel less claustrophobic, a glass roof was fitted to let in the light.

Middle: The lighting was state of the art, because it featured LEDs throughout. As a result, it was incredibly compact but also extremely bright.

Bottom: Thanks to an all-electric drivetrain, the POP's front end could be kept very short, with much of the running gear sitting underneath the car.

Opposite: The POP's interior was an unusual symphony of intense purple and gleaming chrome.

Design

Kia had made great strides with its production cars when the POP appeared in 2010. However, this new concept was still unlike anything ever to grace a Kia showroom. After all, Kia wasn't in the habit of building chrome-colored, 10-foot-long (3-meter) three-seater city cars with an electric drivetrain, oblong-shape side windows, and tilt-forward doors. Considering how many electric car and/or city car concepts have been built over the years, the POP certainly pushed the boundaries.

The most striking thing about the POP was the fact that it was a very short wedge-shape monobox. As Kia explained at the time, it didn't point to the style of the next generation of its cars, but it looked even further into the future. Interestingly, most of the inspiration for the POP came from outside the automotive sphere, with lead designer Gregory Guillaume taking his cues from lightweight, aerodynamic objects, such as gliders and high-speed bikes. As a result, the POP's lines were very clean; instead of rearview mirrors there were tiny rear-facing cameras at the forward base of each door, which relayed pictures to small screens in the cabin.

If the exterior was uncluttered, the interior was even more so. There were no rows of switches or lines of dials to distract. Instead, there was just a single button on the dash, with all other functions, such as the audio, a GPS satellite navigation system, and climate control, operated via an animated touch-screen display.

At a Glance

Country of Manufacture
Germany/France

Engine
Rear-mounted electric motor with 18 kWh lithium polymer gel battery

Power	67 bhp
Torque	140 lb.-ft.

Weights and Measurements

Wheelbase	81 in. (2,055 mm)
Length	118 in. (3,000 mm)
Width	69 in. (1,740 mm)
Height	59 in. (1,490 mm)

Performance

Top speed	88 mph (142 km/h)
Range	100 miles (160 km)
Charging time	6 hours
Fast charge time	30 minutes
CO_2 emissions	0 g/km at tailpipe

Debut:	Paris 2010
Design director:	Peter Schreyer
Chief designer:	Gregory Guillaume

Lamborghini Cala (1995)

Lamborghini set up shop in 1963 and suffered a tumultuous existence until its takeover by Audi in 1999. Constantly teetering on the brink of oblivion, it started to offer junior supercars in 1970 with the arrival of the V8-powered Urraco, which would be developed into the Silhouette later. In turn, this would become the Jalpa; each of these models was designed to take on Ferrari's contemporary V8 model.

Throughout the 1990s there was no junior Lamborghini. The company was too strapped for cash to develop anything, and with only a costly V12-powered supercar on the books (initially the Countach, then the Diablo), Lamborghini would always struggle to expand. However, expansion was what the company needed if it was to survive, and in time the Gallardo would offer Lamborghini the chance to do just that. Unveiled in 2003, the V10-engined Gallardo would go on to become Lamborghini's most successful model ever.

Back in the 1990s, things weren't so rosy. Indonesian-owned Lamborghini had been trying to develop a new junior supercar for years, but it didn't have the cash to see the project through. Thanks to the efforts of the Italdesign studio, however, things started to look a whole lot brighter at the 1995 Geneva Motor Show, when the Cala concept was revealed. Interestingly, despite its Lamborghini badging, the car never appeared on the Lamborghini stand; it was a product of Italdesign, and as such it was shown on the iconic studio's stand.

Here was a fully developed supercar that could be driven at speed, was capable of accommodating two in comfort, and that looked sensational—all that was needed was the cash to put it into production. Which is where things all went wrong.

Above: In many ways, the Cala doesn't look like a concept car—it looks more like a seriously sporty production car. Just this one example was built.

Left to right: However you looked at it, the Cala's proportions worked perfectly, so it's a shame that the company didn't have the resources to put it into production.

Technology

Unlike most concepts, the Cala was intended to be a preview of a usable, road-going supercar, and as such, it was fully driveable. Consequently, there were no technologies incorporated that weren't fully up and running, although the body construction was pretty avant-garde. Featuring a bonded aluminum unibody with carbon-fiber panels, the Cala's construction was cutting edge at the time. Aside from a few very low-volume hypercars, this method of construction was pretty much unknown—it was just too expensive.

As a result, if a production car had emanated from Giorgetto Giugiaro's efforts, the chances are that its construction would have been somewhat less exotic in a bid to keep build costs down. However, whatever method of construction had been chosen, it would have had to offer strength with lightness, which is why Kevlar paneling may well have been the choice for production cars.

Providing performance that was anything but junior, there was a midmounted 3.9-liter V10 that provided a 400 brake horsepower shove—enough to give fearsome acceleration with 180-mile-per-hour (290-kilometer) potential. Until this point there had never been a V10 engine installed in a production road-going Lamborghini, but when the Gallardo arrived in 2003, it would offer exactly that configuration.

The V10's prodigious power was directed solely toward the rear wheels; the Gallardo was four-wheel drive from the outset, although rear-wheel drive models would arrive later.

Top: Lamborghini had never built a production car with a V10 engine before—and it wouldn't do so for almost another decade.

Middle: The Cala was more of a prototype than a concept, which is why it was fully driveable. And it worked wonderfully, too.

Bottom: Everywhere you looked there were scoops, slats, and spoilers. Those pods in the rear fenders are to feed cool air to the midmounted V10.

Design

Lamborghini has never been in the habit of offering cars with anything less than jaw-dropping looks, so the Cala had to offer all the drama of any previous car from the company—and then some. Clearly related to the Diablo, which had already been in production for five years by this point, the Cala featured the classic cab-forward stance of the mid-engined supercar, along with a glut of scoops, slats, and spoilers to keep the engine, brakes, and tires cool. What was unusual was the roofline; for such a short car lengthwise, the Cala was surprisingly tall. However, this height was essential if anybody was going to fit inside. As a result, the Cala was better packaged than most contemporary supercars, including the larger Diablo.

Had the Cala appeared a few years earlier, there may have been pop-up headlights, but by the mid-1990s faired-in lighting was the order of the day for aerodynamic and safety reasons.

What hadn't been seen before in a Lamborghini was the roof treatment; lift-out panels meant the car was a targa design, and because those panels were made of glass, the cabin was constantly bathed in sunlight, opening it further.

As befitted a luxury sports car, the interior was beautifully trimmed in a mixture of leather and suede, featured in claret and tan. Supportive Recaro seats offered comfort and style for those up front; there were two token rear seats, too, but they were suitable for only luggage. After all, Lamborghinis shouldn't be *too* practical.

Italdesign is one of the most talented design houses anywhere, so it was no surprise that it was behind a design as great as this one.

At a Glance

Country of Manufacture
Italy

Engine
Midmounted, normally-aspirated V10

Displacement	238 ci (3,900 cc)
Power	400 bhp

Drivetrain
6-speed manual transmission,
rear-wheel drive

Suspension, Wheels, and Brakes

Front brakes:	12¼-in. (310-mm) ventilated disc
Rear brakes:	12¼-in. (310-mm) ventilated disc
Front tires:	225/40 ZR18
Rear tires:	295/40 ZR18

Weights and Measurements

Curb weight	2,850 lb. (1,293 kg)
Wheelbase	99 in. (2,520 mm)
Length	173 in. (4,389 mm)
Width	75 in. (1,900 mm)
Height	48 in. (1,222 mm)

Performance

0–62 mph	5 seconds
Top speed	180 mph (290 km/h)
Debut:	Geneva 1995
Designer:	Fabrizio Giugiaro

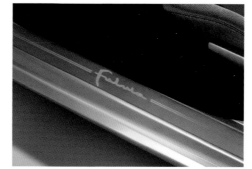

Lancia Fulvietta (2003)

There was a time when Lancia had been incredibly innovative and stylish. Most of its pre- and postwar cars looked superb and featured interesting engineering. One of the most revered is the beautiful front-wheel-drive Fulvia coupé, which debuted in 1965, complete with narrow-angle V4 engine, disc brakes all around, and double-wishbone front suspension. The car would be successful in motorsport, and by the time production ended in 1976, more than 140,000 examples had been built.

However, ever since the Fiat Group acquired the company in 1969, its cars had started to lose their individuality. So when Lancia unveiled its Fulvietta concept at the 2003 Frankfurt Motor Show, it looked like the company was finally finding its way after many years in the wilderness. Lancia had gone off the rails with the demise of the Integrale in the 1990s and had never really managed to come up with anything to inspire buyers. Here was a car that took the beautiful lines of the Fulvia and improved on them.

All was not what it seemed. When the Fulvietta was unveiled, Lancia was noncommittal about its prospects of making production. The press went wild over the concept, and potential buyers lined up with checkbooks in hand. However, Lancia bosses couldn't make up their minds about whether or not to build the car, although it was generally agreed that this was the best-looking machine to come from the company in years—if not decades.

In the end, Lancia elected not to build the car; the company decided that it would cost too much to develop and build relative to its sales potential. As if that weren't bad enough, thanks to the Fiat Group's acquisition of Chrysler in 2011, in some markets Lancias became nothing more than rebadged Chryslers. This may have saved Lancia a pile of cash in development costs, but it did little for a brand that was once so great.

Above: How could Lancia not have put this into production? One of the best-looking concept cars ever built, the Fulvietta is one of the all-time missed opportunities.

Left to right: There was no mistaking which classic sired the Fulvietta, but it didn't matter that the concept was unashamedly retro—it just worked wonderfully.

Technology

The whole point of the Fulvietta was that it could have gone into production with minimal changes. Sure, some of the detailing may have had to be watered down, but the concept was based on tried-and-tested components taken from the Lancia parts catalog. There was a 1.7-liter four-cylinder gasoline engine transversely mounted up front.

The 140 brake horsepower on tap was fed to the front wheels, just as in the original Fulvia; such a layout ensured low production costs, better packaging, and more sure-footed (if perhaps slightly less entertaining) handling. Channeling that power was a five-speed manual transmission, although the Fiat Group is no stranger to more unusual transmissions, such as semiautomatic units with sequential gear selection.

The Fulvietta's construction was also deliberately kept simple to maximize its chances of becoming a commercial reality. The unibody was made of welded steel, while the panels were all made of aluminum. The latter helped to keep the Fulvietta's weight down to just 2,183 pounds (990 kilograms), but it's probable that any production car's paneling would have had to be made from steel to keep production costs down. However, it's also probable that Lancia would have been able to incorporate some plastic panels—items such as the hood or trunk lid. As a result, while any production Fulvietta was unlikely to have remained below the magic 1-ton (907-kilogram) curb weight, with a little ingenuity and imagination, the final figure shouldn't have been much higher.

Top: An update of the classic Fulvia dash, the Fulvietta's dashboard featured instruments in nacelles along with a chrome-trimmed three-spoke steering wheel.

Middle: There was an unashamedly 1970s-inspired cabin full of brown leather and Alcantara, plus wood trim galore, and it looked great.

Bottom: The Fulvietta was a fully functioning prototype, which is why it featured a standard production engine and transmission.

Opposite: This design sketch documents the evolutions of the Fulvietta.

Design

The key thing about the Fulvietta's design was that it borrowed heavily from the Fulvia coupé that Lancia built between 1965 and 1976. That car had featured very slender pillars to produce a light and airy cabin; this new model was no different. Indeed, the Fulvietta was essentially the original car updated using twenty-first century technologies and design details.

There was flush glazing along with much tighter build tolerances, so the end result was a car that looked of a much higher quality and was more modern and far more aerodynamically efficient. Also, while the dimensions and proportions hardly varied between the old car and the new, the track was wider for greater stability.

The interior was just as wonderfully thought out as the exterior. While brown would usually look dated, Lancia used it effectively both inside and out. The dash was once again clearly inspired by the original Fulvia, so there was a wood finish and some very simply laid out switch gear and displays—it looked stylish and retro instead of contrived.

There was room for just two occupants, each of whom was provided with a bucket seat; the space behind was given over exclusively to luggage. Of course, there was a trunk, too, for extra carrying capacity; the show car came with a set of handmade leather luggage, produced specially by Trussardi, to make the best possible use of the available trunk space.

At a Glance

Country of Manufacture
Italy

Engine
Front-mounted, normally aspirated four-cylinder gas

Displacement	107 ci (1,747 cc)
Power	140 bhp

Drivetrain
Five-speed manual transmission, front-wheel drive

Suspension, Wheels, and Brakes
Front suspension: MacPherson struts with coil springs and lower wishbones
Rear suspension: Longitudinal arms with antiroll bar
Front brakes: Ventilated discs
Rear brakes: Solid discs

Weights and Measurements
Curb weight:	2,183 lb. (990 kg)
Wheelbase:	92 in. (2,330 mm)
Length:	156 in. (3,975 mm)
Width:	62 in. (1,570 mm)
Height:	51 in. (1,300 mm)

Performance
0–62 mph	8.5 seconds
Top speed	132 mph (212 km/h)
Debut:	Frankfurt 2003
Designed by:	Lancia Centro Stile

Land Rover Range Stormer (2004)

Amazingly, despite the first Land Rover appearing in 1948, it wasn't until 2004 that the company produced its first concept. If you're looking for a classic case of how concept cars are watered down before reaching the showroom, here's the perfect example. While the Range Rover Sport was the production version of the Stormer, the concept car's amazing lines were largely lost in the transition.

Despite the relative disappointment of the final production design, at least the Range Stormer was very clearly a product of Land Rover, with many of its styling cues harking back to the first Range Rover of 1970. However, while many of the styling elements looked back, the technology incorporated in the Stormer was very much about the future.

Crucially, the Stormer signaled a future for Land Rover that was more about on-road performance than off-road—not that the Sport would be a lame duck in the rough. It was clear that buyers of premium SUVs wanted the looks and image without actually having any intention of ever going off-road. As a result, Land Rover focused its energies on creating a superlative 4x4 with on-road capabilities better than anything it had ever built before—but it would still be able to leave all rivals standing when it came to off-roading.

While it offered a sneak preview of Land Rover's forthcoming baby Range Rover, and some of the technologies it incorporated, more important, the Range Stormer also showcased the all-new platform that Land Rover had created for its new premium SUVs, such as the Discovery and Sport. It would prove to be a fantastic move, because the production car arrived on the crest of a wave, at a time when buyers couldn't get enough of premium SUVs. However, that still didn't stop Ford from off-loading one of the jewels in its crown, with Land Rover later being snapped up by Indian outfit Tata.

Above: With its shallow glasshouse and three-door configuration, the Stormer looked seriously sporty—especially for an off-roader.

Left to right: The metallic-orange paintwork helped set off the lines, while there was gorgeous detailing all over; grilles, badges, wheels, and lights were all neatly styled.

Technology

Technologically, there was nothing in the Range Stormer that couldn't be translated into a similar road car—and indeed, when the showroom-ready Range Rover Sport appeared soon after, it incorporated just about everything that had featured in the concept.

Because the original Range Rover had been a workhorse, the platform on which the Range Stormer was based was designed for go-anywhere ability. The Range Stormer was much more about on-road driving pleasure, which is why the all-new platform on which it was based was biased much more toward high-speed handling and refinement.

Powering the Range Stormer was the same supercharged 4-liter V8 more usually found under the hood of assorted Jaguars, such as the XJR and XKR. Tuned to produce 370 brake horsepower with an equally monstrous 387 lb.-ft. of torque, the gas-fed V8 was conventional but welcome; it offered power and pull for high-speed cruising or low-speed mud-plugging.

To show that, as with any Land Rover product, the Range Stormer could be used on rugged terrains, it previewed a new technology that would be fitted as standard to all high-end Land Rovers: terrain response. This offered a selection of terrains, such as sand, rocks, and snow, which could be chosen from the dash-mounted dial. By choosing the appropriate terrain, the engine mapping, transmission shift points, suspension height and firmness, along with the brake bias, could all be tailored to suit.

Top: The cabin was filled with natural materials, especially oak, leather, and aluminum, with the latter used effectively to brighten up the interior.

Middle: There were four individual seats fitted, each one constructed from a single hide; their design was inspired by the Möbius strip.

Bottom: The four-spoke steering wheel looked like it would survive a nuclear bomb, because it was basically a solid billet of aluminum with a rim.

Design

While the technology was carried over largely unchanged from concept to production car, the design was watered down just a little too much for comfort. Indeed, there were many who felt underwhelmed by the Range Rover Sport after the Range Stormer had promised so much.

Land Rover would never offer a three-door version of the Range Rover Sport, while the much lower roofline of the Stormer made it look as though the car had been the subject of a roof chop. Of course, the roofline had to be raised for production cars, otherwise practicality would have suffered too much, but there was no doubt that the Stormer lost a lot of its visual appeal in the translation from concept to road car.

There were plenty of Range Rover styling cues in evidence, however, such as the trademark "floating roof," initially seen on the first cars that went on sale in 1970. The bluff front end featured a deep front air dam, and those jewel-effect stepped headlights were a Land Rover trademark. The glasshouse was narrow and emphasized by the high waistline to give the Stormer a very tough look.

The roof was made completely of glass, to allow light to flood into the cabin, while the electrically powered doors were a two-piece affair that Land Rover dubbed "blade and runner." The upper half hinged up and forward, while the lower portion dropped to provide a step up into the cabin. Unsurprisingly, by the time the Stormer made production, it was fitted with conventional doors.

It wasn't just the exterior that was watered down; in common with many concepts, the cabin was scaled back even more. It featured four individual seats—their distinctive design was inspired by the concept of the Möbius strip—and the deep brown saddle leather facings were cut from a single hide.

At a Glance

Country of Manufacture
UK

Engine
Front-mounted, supercharged gas V8

Displacement	244 ci (3,996 cc)
Power	370 bhp
Torque	387 lb.-ft.

Drivetrain
Six-speed automatic transmission, four-wheel drive

Suspension, Wheels, and Brakes
Front suspension: Air suspension with double wishbones with coil springs

Rear suspension: Air suspension with double wishbones with coil springs

Wheels: 22-in. (559-mm) forged alloys front and rear

Weights and Measurements

Curb weight	5,512 lb. (2,500 kg)
Wheelbase	108 in. (2,750 mm)
Length	186 in. (4,730 mm)
Width	76 in. (1,940 mm)
Height	71 in. (1,810 mm)

Performance

0–62 mph	7.5 seconds approx.
Top speed	140 mph approx.

Debut:	Detroit 2004
Design director:	Geoff Upex

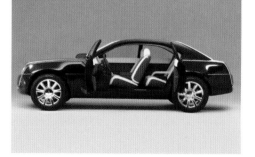

Lincoln Navicross (2003)

It all used to be so simple. Cars were sedans, convertibles, or occasionally they were station wagons. However, something changed, and every new car that came along had to pioneer a new niche, ideally taking the best from at least two existing segments and creating something better. Welcome to the world of the crossover, mixing as many segments as possible, no matter how diverse.

The Lincoln Navicross was one of these crossovers, perhaps looking like a large, luxury sedan, but being much more than that. Designed to be a sporty alternative to a full-blown sport-utility vehicle, this showstopper was first seen at the 2003 Detroit Motor Show. After the appearance of the sinister-looking Lincoln Sentinel at the same event seven years earlier, it was clear that Ford's upscale U.S. division was set to take a new design direction. Although American cars hadn't been especially curvaceous since the 1950s, these new cars were taking the hard edges to extremes—standing too close to either the Sentinel or the Navicross could lead to you cutting yourself.

While the Sentinel was seriously sharp (literally and metaphorically) with its exterior design, the Navicross wasn't as extreme. The third in a series of concepts, after the 2001 MK9 and the 2002 Continental, the Navicross offered a preview of what Lincoln's showroom products would look like in the near future.

Some of Lincoln's concepts of this period were little more than thinly disguised previews of production cars, and, unfortunately, the Navicross concept went nowhere, which is a shame. While any niche that has yet to be created and exploited is probably a niche too far, in the case of the Navicross, you get the distinct impression when you look at it that something like this would probably sell well. Maybe one day.

Above: Lincoln had never offered anything like this before; it was a sedan, hatchback, and off-roader all rolled into one.

Left to right: There was no mistaking from which country the Navicross hailed; that glitzy grille and those wide rear lights were pure Americana.

Technology

One of the key technologies fitted to the Navicross was its height-adjustable air suspension. When combined with the permanent four-wheel drive plus adaptive traction control, ground clearance could be increased so drivers could undertake proper off-roading. When the car was just cruising, the height could be dropped so the car's dynamics weren't compromised.

Plenty of power and torque were also on tap, and both were provided by a boosted 4.2-liter V8, which drove all four wheels via a five-speed semiautomatic transmission, the latter incorporating "fuzzy logic" technology that allowed for the car's brain to sense the driving style and terrain, and adjust the gear-shift points to suit.

It's probable that the V8 installed would have provided at least 300 brake horsepower, if not closer to 400, so the Navicross needed a pretty talented chassis to cope. That air suspension with automatic self-leveling would have helped get the power down without fuss, and the brakes were seriously beefy, too—there was a Brembo system fitted for ultimate stopping power. Ventilated discs measuring 14 inches (355 millimeters) all around were backed up with antilock technology plus electronic brake force distribution. And to leave onlookers in no doubt to the Navicross's potential, there were 20-inch (508-millimeter) alloy wheels all around.

Although the Navicross's front end was bulky, its surface area was reduced because of its use of a new type of lighting technology. By using a fiber-optic ribbon with a remote light source, the car's front overhang was reduced, along with its overall length, in a bid to make the car more agile.

Top: The dashboard was packed with all the latest technology, as you'd expect from Ford's most upscale marque.

Middle: There was seating just for four, and going by this photograph, there wasn't much room for those in the back.

Bottom: With its lift-up tailgate, fold-down rear panel, and fold-flat rear seats, the Navicross was decently practical, while still being luxurious.

Design

It was hard to pigeonhole the Navicross's design, because it featured a sedanlike silhouette but also a hatchback for added practicality. And thanks to that adjustable suspension, its ride height could make it appear as though it was a conventional sedan or more like an SUV. This was one confusing machine.

It was around this time that rear-hinged back doors were coming back into fashion, largely thanks to the appearance of Mazda's RX-Evolv concept in 1999, which would later go into production as the RX-8. Sure enough, the Navicross featured rear doors of the same design, with the obligatory lack of a B-pillar to go with it.

Another modern take on a traditional theme was the use of brushed alloy for the external brightwork in place of the more usual chrome. Particularly striking was the fillet of aluminum that indicated the swage line, which ran for the entire length of the car—and very neatly it also disguised the door handles along the way.

Predictably, the interior was every bit as luxurious as the exterior. As soon as the doors opened, the car's composite safety frame was discreetly displayed, while the cabin was trimmed tastefully in terra-cotta and cream leather. With glass roof panels, the cabin was bathed in ambient light during the day, making it feel much lighter and more airy.

Maintaining the understated theme, the dash was kept as uncluttered as possible; the clean look was helped by a pair of large touch-screen displays—one in front of the driver and another in front of the passenger. The former displayed information relating to the car, such as speed, engine temperature, fuel level, and so on. The passenger's screen was for Internet access along with control of the navigation system, and it could be set up using voice control or the built-in mouse. If this wasn't enough, there was a third screen in the center console, through which the climate control and entertainment system could be controlled.

At a Glance

Country of Manufacture
USA

Engine
Front-mounted, supercharged gas V8

Displacement   4.2 liters

Drivetrain
Five-speed semiautomatic transmission, four-wheel drive

Suspension, Wheels, and Brakes
Air-sprung height-adjustable suspension all around

Front wheels/tires: 20 x 9-in. (508 x 229-mm) alloy wheels with 255/50 R20 Continental all-terrain tires

Rear wheels/tires: 20 x 9-in. (508 x 229-mm) alloy wheels with 255/50 R20 Continental all-terrain tires

Front brakes: 14-in. (355-mm) ventilated discs with four-piston calipers

Rear brakes: 14-in. (355-mm) ventilated discs with four-piston calipers

Weights and Measurements

Wheelbase	114 in. (2,900 mm)
Length	187 in. (4,741 mm)
Width	73 in. (1,862 mm)
Height	59 in. (1,500 mm)

Debut:	Detroit 2003
Design director:	Gerry McGovern

Lincoln C Concept (2009)

Rewind to the 1950s, 1960s, and 1970s, and you'd struggle to find a car in Lincoln's lineup that didn't have the size and weight of an aircraft carrier. However, times change, and by the twenty-first century, a spacious cabin and excellent practicality no longer meant a car proportioned like a supertanker. Indeed, being the same kind of size as Ford's then-current Focus, the C Concept was pretty radical for a company that had always assumed that biggest means best—and whose buyers had always reckoned that for ultimate luxury, size mattered.

Naturally, the key reason for this downsizing was greater efficiency, but the fact of the matter was by this stage in the car's development, modern packaging meant even small cars could offer big-car comfort, space, safety, and equipment while using up far fewer precious resources. Buyers also were now used to the idea that, in many cases, smaller can mean better; Lincoln cited examples of great product designs, such as cell phones and MP3 players, which delivered all the benefits of much bulkier products but in smaller packages.

To illustrate just how far car packaging had come since the 1960s, Lincoln claimed that the C Concept offered the interior space of its 1961 Continental—and all that was required was a 2-inch (508-mm) increase in width over the typical car in the class. To put that into perspective, the C Concept was around 14 feet 7 inches (4,445 millimeters) long and 5 feet 10 inches (1,770 millimeters) wide compared with the 1961 Continental at 18 feet 9 inches (5,400 millimeters) long and 6 feet 7 inches (2,000 millimeters) wide. Now that's progress.

Above: Just how far can you stretch a brand? Or in the case of the C Concept, just how far can you squash it? Lincoln had never made a car this small before.

Left to right: Despite its compact dimensions, the idea of the C Concept was that it still offered huge amounts of interior space along with ample luxury, largely thanks to a generous girth.

Technology

While many of the C Concept's contemporaries were showcasing the latest in power trains and transmissions, there were no such advances here. There was no hybrid or electric propulsion; instead, power was provided by Ford's latest 1.6-liter Ecoboost gasoline engine, driving the front wheels via a six-speed Powershift dual-clutch transmission. Offering an impressive 180 brake horsepower and 180 lb.-ft. of torque, the small and relatively light C Concept had strong performance while still giving 43 miles per hour on a U.S. gallon (69 kilometers per 3.8 liters), or 51 miles per gallon (82 kilometers per 3.8 liters) on the European combined cycle; many of the C's predecessors would have struggled to achieve 20 percent of that.

While there was nothing to get excited about where the C Concept's propulsion was concerned, Lincoln did shout about the driver information and in-car connectivity systems. The basis of the C's connectivity capabilities was Ford's signature HMI (human-machine interface). This intelligent interface was designed to make useful and relevant information and functionality immediately available to the driver in a way that was logical, easy to use, and completely integrated.

The key to Ford's HMI was how and where information was displayed. All car-related information, for example, was shown to the left of the speedometer, such as fuel economy, trip information, and vehicle diagnostics. Passenger-related functions, such as the audio, climate, navigation, and phone, appeared to the right of the instrument cluster. The system's integrated platform offered intuitive methods of information control, such as steering wheel switches, touch screens, and voice activation, any of which could be used by the driver.

Top: To make the cabin feel as big as possible, it was trimmed throughout in very pale materials; it was a ploy that worked.

Middle: The hubless multifunction steering wheel was a stroke of genius, although perhaps a little too radical for conservative Lincoln buyers.

Bottom: Also in a bid to open up the cabin, there were glass panels in the roof to let natural light flood in.

Design

When design director Peter Horbury briefed his designers to create the C Concept, their target was to come up with a midsize car that offered both presence and elegance. Whether or not they succeeded is up to you, but it would be easy to argue that the C looked pretty slick from most angles.

The C's short length meant the wheels had to be pushed out to the corners to give a decent ride along with ample cabin space. The short overhangs resulted in a silhouette that was unmistakeable, but while the C was far more compact than any previous Lincoln, it also incorporated the key iconic elements from the company's DNA: sheer surfaces bounded by defined creases, a cantilevered roof extending from a strong C-pillar, that classic double-fender chrome grille, and also those full-width taillights and brightwork.

Concepts without a B-pillar had started to become popular by this point, but for Lincoln it was no mere styling affectation; it was a direct reference to its landmark 1961 Continental. With forward-hinged front doors and rear-hinged back ones, entry and exit was simplicty itself.

Meanwhile, instead of side-mounted mirrors, there were rearview cameras on each side along with blind spot detection technologies. An all-glass roof illuminated a cabin that was something of a masterpiece. The cabin looked more like the living room of a contemporary urban pad than the inside of a car, and everywhere you looked there were high-quality materials, such as wood and metal, ambient lighting, and jewel-like chrome details.

The interior's all-white color palette—from roof to seats to floor—was especially eye-catching. Subtle chrome accents on the seats, instrument panel, door panels, and floor glimmered, while the light gray wood veneer contrasted with the white leather on the instrument panel and door panels. It may not have been practical, but it sure looked good.

At a Glance

Country of Manufacture
USA

Engine
Front-mounted, turbocharged
four-cylinder gas

Displacement	1.6 liters
Power	180 bhp
Torque	180 lb.-ft.

Drivetrain
Six-speed semiautomatic transmission, front-wheel drive

Suspension, Wheels, and Brakes
Not disclosed

Weights and Measurements

Wheelbase	103 in. (2,610 mm)
Length	175 in. (4,445 mm)
Width	70 in. (1,770 mm)

Performance

Fuel consumption	51 mpg
Debut:	Detroit 2009
Design director:	Peter Horbury

Maybach Exelero (2005)

While it looks like a refugee from a Batman movie, the Exelero was never designed for a starring role on the silver screen. Instead, it was designed as a mobile test bed for high-speed tires, bankrolled by tire maker Fulda and based on the platform of the Maybach 57 limousine. This wasn't the first time that Fulda had teamed up with the Maybach marque, nor was it the first time that the tire maker had built a vehicle for the purpose of demonstrating its products. Back in 1938, Fulda commissioned Frankfurt-based coach builders Dörr & Schreck to build a one-of-a-kind version of the Maybach SW38 to enable high-speed tire testing on Germany's autobahns. That car was completed in July 1938—just before the outbreak of World War II. During the war, the car disappeared and was never seen again.

In the meantime, Fulda commissioned a madly modified Porsche 911 (by Gemballa) to demonstrate its 1996 range. When an all-new lineup of tires was unveiled in 2005, the company wanted to pull out all the stops and commission something unique. The Maybach marque had been revived by this point, and Fulda teamed up with DaimlerChrysler, custodians of the Maybach brand, to build a showstopping car that had as much go as it did show. However, time was tight; the plan was to unveil the car in just two years, at the 2005 Frankfurt Motor Show, having already run high-speed tests beforehand. Two years may sound like a lot of time, but for a fully running, record-breaking one-of-a-kind car to be built in that time is a challenge. The solution was in building the chassis, interior, and body shell separately and concurrently, with the work being undertaken by speciality coach builder Stola in Italy.

The Exelero was completed by April 2005, ready for high-speed testing. It had been honed in the wind tunnel and refined ever further, but finally, in May 2005, the Exelero clinched the world record for a car running on standard tires. At just over 219 miles (352 kilometers) per hour, it was capable of maxing Fulda's all-new road car tire.

Above: Understatement isn't a word that's in Maybach's dictionary, but even so, the Exelero was a crazy concept in every way.

Left to right: The Exelero looked satanic from every angle, partly because of its black paintwork, while the proportions were also menacing.

Technology

The whole Exelero exercise was carried out so that Fulda could show off its new Carat Exelero range of tires—the largest of which had a diameter of 23 inches (584 millimeters). The tires were capable of running at speeds of up to 219 miles (352 kilometers) per hour, so the Exelero's top speed needed to match this. While the standard Maybach range was hardly lacking in terms of available performance, something special would have to be done to achieve the level of speed that Fulda required.

In a bid to extract as many horses as possible from the twin-turbo V12 power plant, its capacity was increased from 5.6 to 5.9 liters. That liberated an extra 150 brake horsepower or so, taking the tally up to 700 brake horsepower, which was enough to take the Exelero up to its 219-miles-per-hour (352-kilometer) target speed. However, it wasn't capable of attaining such velocities in the form shown here. To improve aerodynamics, the wheels were enclosed with paneling—boosting the top speed by around 2½ miles (4 kilometers) per hour.

Despite the enormous power output, only the rear wheels were driven; four-wheel drive would have added too much weight to a car that already tipped the scales at a hefty 5,864 pounds (2,660 kilograms). There were vented discs all around, each equipped with four-piston calipers; naturally there was antilock and ESP circuitry, too. And just to make sure that the power was transmitted to the road safely as possible, there was double-wishbone suspension up front and a multilink rear design.

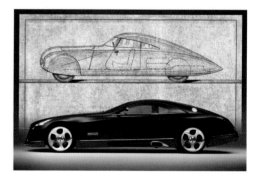

Top: The interior was a let down after that crazy exterior, largely because much of the dash was carried over from Maybach's production cars.

Middle: The Exelero came about because of Fulda's requirement for a car that could do 219 mph (352 km/h) to demonstrate its new road tire.

Bottom: When compared with one of the original streamlined Maybachs from the 1930s, it's easy to see where the inspiration came from for the Exelero's exterior design.

Opposite: This image shows how the Exelero's design echoed that of the original 1930s' Maybach.

Design

While the mechanical side was clearly crucial to getting the car up to the required velocities, its design and construction were also important. To come up with a suitably menacing look, Fulda teamed up with the students of Pforzheim Polytechnic's Department of Transport Design. It wasn't the first time the two had collaborated—in the mid-1990s they had teamed up to create a futuristic truck to showcase Fulda's products. This time around, the work of 24-year-old Fredrik Burchhardt was chosen as the basis for the project; his design was just what Fulda reckoned it needed to grab plenty of column inches in the world's media.

Despite the Exelero being even longer than the Maybach 57 that donated its platform, it featured seating for just two people. Italian specialty vehicle maker Stola built the car at its base in Turin, and by the summer of 2005, the car was ready to be unveiled. Although there were few definite requirements for the exterior styling (the main one being that no retro suggestions would even get out of the starting blocks), there were some very specific demands where the interior was concerned. On the list of required materials were natural leather, neoprene, and coated punched aluminum sheet, along with carbon fiber finished in glossy black and red. Whether it looked classy or like a boudoir is a matter of interpretation.

At a Glance

Country of Manufacture
Germany/Italy

Engine
Front-mounted twin-turbo gas V12

Displacement	360 ci (5,908 cc)
Power	700 bhp
Torque	752 lb.-ft.

Drivetrain
Five-speed automatic transmission, rear-wheel drive

Suspension, Wheels, and Brakes
Front suspension: Double wishbones with coil springs

Rear suspension: Multilink rear axle alloy wheels front and rear, measuring 23 x 11 in. (584 x 279 mm), with Fulda Carat Exelero 315/25 ZR23 tires

Front brakes: Four-piston 15-in. (376-mm) ventilated discs

Rear brakes: Four-piston 14-in. (355-mm) ventilated discs

Weights and Measurements

Curb weight	5,864 lb. (2,660 kg)
Wheelbase	133 in. (3,390 mm)
Length	232 in. (5,890 mm)
Width	84 in. (2,140 mm)
Height	55 in. (1,390 mm)

Performance

0–62 mph	4.4 seconds
Top speed	219 mph (352 km/h)

Debut:	Frankfurt 2005
Designer:	Fredrik Burchhardt

Mazda Nagare (2006)

Over the years, Mazda has produced some of the best-looking concept cars ever. Yet few are only thought of as seminal works; it always seems to be the Italian design houses that are credited with producing the landmark concepts. When it comes to missed opportunities, you've only got to look at certain models, such as the RX-01 and MX-02, to see that Mazda has some great concept designs in its past.

Unlike many carmakers, Mazda doesn't trade on its past, although it has a lot more heritage than you might think; instead, it's always looking to the future in a bid to constantly reinvent itself. And that was exactly the purpose of the Nagare—to show a new design language that would come to define Mazda's production cars as well as a series of great-looking concepts.

The new design language was called Nagare, the Japanese word for "flow," and it was only fitting that the first car in the series would be known as the Nagare. The idea behind this new design language was that it would be the embodiment of motion—so even when stationary, any car designed with this language in mind would look as though it was moving. Such a notion is clichéd, of course; for decades that's been the aim of car designers around the globe—to look as though a car is doing 100 miles (160 kilometers) per hour even when it's standing still. Whether or not you could successfully argue that Mazda achieved its aim with any of the concepts in this series is a moot point, but one thing is undeniable: they all looked sensational.

Upon the Nagare's unveiling, Franz von Holzhausen, Mazda's North American design director, explained: "We're looking well down the road with Nagare. We want to suggest where Mazda design will be in 2020. We develop these ideas to demonstrate what we really intend to build and sell." So here's to 2020, when it's likely that Mazda's factories will go into meltdown because of the demand for cars that look like the Nagare.

Above: One day, all family cars will look this fabulous. Or maybe not. But one can hope that design as cool as this will eventually be the norm.

Left to right: To maximize cabin space, the Nagare's rear end was cut off very abruptly, while the front end was arrow shaped for optimum aerodynamics.

Technology

As the first in a series of design-led concepts, Mazda didn't offer any information on any of the techologies the Nagare might contain, except for some sketchy details of a potential power train. Indeed, it's likely that the Nagare wasn't even a runner; this wasn't intended to be a technological tour de force, but a stylistic one.

With the car supposedly scheduled for an introduction more than a decade after it was first revealed, it was a given that propulsion systems would have changed substantially—possibly beyond all recognition. Despite this, Mazda suggested that the Nagare would be powered by a hydrogen-fueled rotary engine. The Nagare would be unique; nobody else was still working with rotary engines, although hydrogen as a fuel source was becoming increasingly popular. In some cases, such as with BMW, hydrogen was used to fuel generally conventional internal combustion engines, while many other carmakers were using it in conjunction with fuel cells—a technology that was still at least a decade into the future for production cars, when the Nagare was unveiled.

The attraction of hydrogen was easy to see; it's the most abundant element in the universe and it burns very cleanly, with the only by-product being water. However, it's also generally available only by electrolizing water, which in itself consumes a lot of energy—and handling and storing hydrogen could also be a tricky process.

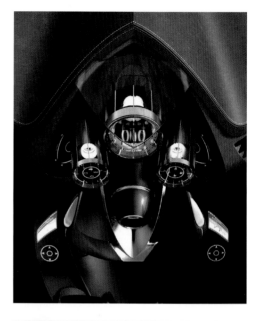

Top: In keeping with that futuristic exterior, there was an equally forward-thinking interior with a dashboard straight out of the twenty-second century.

Middle: As well as a steering wheel that looked as though it came from a jet fighter, there were TV screens for those in the back.

Bottom: Instead of each occupant getting their own door, there was a single dihedral/gull-wing opening for each side.

Design

Mazda's design team started by studying motion and the effect it has on natural surroundings: how wind shapes sand in the desert, how water moves across the ocean floor, and the look of lava flowing down a mountainside. Natural motion registers an impression in your brain and that's what the team hoped to capture with the Nagare design language.

Once the team started sketching ideas, members weren't surprised to find similar quests underway in other product design disciplines. For example, they found examples of motion influencing the shape and surface of furniture, architecture, and even clothing, so they knew they were onto something with their attempt to introduce the discipline to automotive design.

Access to the four-seat interior was provided by two double-length doors that hinged forward and up like the wings of a butterfly. The driver was centrally located, as in a single-seat racing car, for optimum control and visibility. With the driver positioned under the highest portion of the roof, there was ample headroom with a comfortably reclined backrest. Meanwhile, the rear compartment was a wraparound lounge offering relaxed accommodation for up to three passengers. The central front seat and expansive door opening offered easy entry to the surprisingly roomy interior, and while this looked like a pretty radical solution, it actually made a lot of sense—although it would have come at a price, of course.

The rotary engine allowed for a lower front end than normal, thanks to the rotary power plant's inherently compact dimensions. The use of LED lighting at the front also helped with that lower, while at the rear it allowed for a more characterful taillight display—not that the Nagare needed it. This was a car that was packed with character from bumper to bumper.

At a Glance

Country of Manufacture
Japan/USA

Engine
Front-mounted, hydrogen-powered rotary (proposed)

Drivetrain
Likely to be a semiautomatic or sequential manual

Debut: Los Angeles 2006
Design head: Franz von Holzhausen
Design director: Laurens van den Ackers

Mazda Taiki (2008)

Concepts are supposed to push the boundaries both stylistically and technically, but even some of the most forward-thinking examples seem conventional next to the Mazda Taiki, which looked nothing less than stunning when it was unveiled late in 2007. Indeed, it's one of those concepts that will always look stunning because production road cars are highly unlikely to ever resemble anything so beautiful, thanks to safety and packaging constraints.

The Taiki was the fourth in a series of concepts from Mazda, which followed its then-new design language of Nagare. The Taiki followed up the Nagare, Ryuga, and Hakaze design studies that had appeared over the previous year or so, each one featuring a design that embodied movement, with most of the styling references inspired by nature—things like waves, sand dunes, and lava flows. The result here was even more stunning than in any of the previous studies, which is why it's worth revisiting the theme.

When it was unveiled, Mazda claimed that the Taiki was potentially an early view of what a future sports car from the company might look like. While anything so extreme was always going to be unlikely, Mazda hasn't been afraid to build some unusually designed cars in the past, most notably the final RX-7 and the RX-8, the latter with its rear-hinged back doors.

The whole point of the Taiki was to create a driver's car that was also aerodynamically efficient. To that aim, this front-engined, rear-wheel-drive sports car was ultraslippery and featured just two seats; trying to fit any more into such a compact shape would have led to the proportions being completely wrong. As it was, Mazda's team got things just about perfect.

Above: The Taiki was full of organic references, from its shape to the lighting. The rear lighting was especially beautiful.

Left to right: All of the concepts in Mazda's Nagare series were incredibly striking, but the Taiki was arguably the most amazingly styled car of the lot.

Technology

In the 1960s, it looked as though the next big leap in car technology was the arrival of the Wankel rotary engine. More compact and smoother than a conventional piston engine, it caused many carmakers to buy licenses to use the technology, only to find that the rotary engine was inherently thirsty and unreliable. Only one carmaker persisted with the design, making it dependable and less thirsty—and that was Mazda.

By sticking with rotary engines, Mazda has been able to introduce cars with much lower front ends than generally seen elsewhere, and this was typified by the Taiki, which featured the next generation of Wankel design—a power plant that was smoother, more efficient, and more powerful than ever before.

Inside, the key technology on show was Mazda's human-machine interface, or HMI. The purpose of this was to make it easier for the driver to control the car, while it also incorporated a series of cutting-edge safety features. The key to it all was a steering wheel hub that allowed the driver to control all of the Taiki's key functions without having to lift his hands from the wheel. As if this wasn't enough, the steering wheel also featured various displays more usually seen in the dashboard, so how Mazda expected to fit an air bag to the wheel is anybody's guess. However, that's the whole idea of a concept sometimes—not to focus on the practicalities too much.

Top: The flowing themes continued inside, with the dash displays as well as the structure of the dashboard—and even the steering wheel.

Middle: The overhead view is even more dramatic than the profile, with the windshield flowing into the roof to lighten up the whole cabin.

Bottom: Unusually, one side of the Taiki was tailored in white while the other was finished in black. It looked odd, but somehow it worked.

Opposite: This early model shows the concept at its barest—and it's still striking.

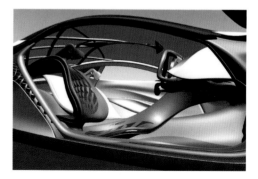

Design

The Taiki took its name from the Japanese word for "atmosphere," which according to Mazda is what wraps around the earth with its protective mantle. So the cornerstones of the Taiki's exterior design were protection, environmental sustainability, and movement. While it would be easy to dismiss all this as marketing hype, what matters is that the result was sensational—a car that looked like nothing else before or since.

More intriguingly, the challenge given to the Taiki's styling team was to create a design that visually expressed the flow of air, inspired by the image of a pair of *Hagoramo*—the flowing robes that enable a celestial maiden to fly in Japanese legend—floating down from the sky. Although it sounds as though the stylists were smoking something strange, when you look at the Taiki you can see how it all adds up; its bodywork really does look like robes flowing in the wind.

Neat touches included lighting only visible when illuminated, alloy wheels inspired by the fan blades of a jet engine, and an interior just as slick as the exterior. Bizarrely, the interior was inspired by Koinobori, or carp-shaped wind socks used to celebrate the Japanese Tango no Sekku day. This continued the airflow theme, and, unusually, the driver's side was colored white while the passenger's side was all white, too. If you looked at it too long, chances were it would cause your brain to spin . . .

At a Glance

Country of Manufacture
Japan

Engine
Front-mounted, normally aspirated rotary

Drivetrain
Seven-speed dual-clutch semiautomatic transmission, rear-wheel drive

Suspension, Wheels, and Brakes
Front suspension: Double wishbone with coil springs and shock absorbers

Rear suspension: Double wishbone with coil springs and shock absorbers

Tires: 22 in. (559 mm) front and rear

Weights and Measurements

Wheelbase	118 in. (3,000 mm)
Length	182 in. (4,620 mm)
Width	77 in. (1,950 mm)
Height	49 in. (1,240 mm)
Drag coefficient	0.25

Debut:	Tokyo 2007
Lead designer:	Yamada Atsuhiko
Design director:	Laurens van den Acker

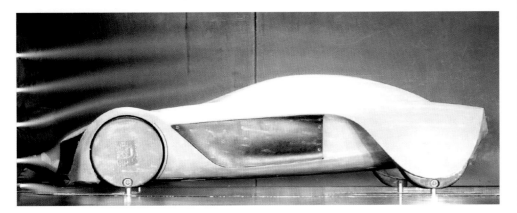

Mercedes F400 Carving (2001)

Few carmakers are as conservative as Mercedes, but every so often this huge German conglomerate lets its hair down and produces something so utterly strange that it shows there's a great sense of humor somewhere inside the corporation. However, as with all great design studies, there was a serious side to the F400 Carving, too; it incorporated some technologies that were wacky to say the least, but that could also be refined to make Mercedes' production cars better in a multitude of ways.

The F400 Carving followed in the tire tracks of the F100 of 1991, the F200 Imagination study of 1996, and the F300 Lifejet, which was unveiled in 1997. While the F100 was a radical MPV and the F200 a technologically advanced coupé, the F300 was a three-wheeler sports car unlike anything ever to come out of the Mercedes factory. So, in some ways, the F400 Carving was a bit less radical than what had gone before, but not much.

As with the previous concepts, the F400 showcased radical chassis technologies aimed at producing cars more dynamically capable and safer than ever before—no mean feat when you consider what a great record Mercedes has in the latter area.

As well as those radical chassis technologies, the F400 also experimented with lightweight materials in its construction, cutting-edge design elements, and some features that were so advanced that when the F400 was unveiled, it wouldn't have been able to be driven on public roads because legislation was still to be passed that would allow the car to be legal on the road. In the event, some of those technologies would go on to be fitted to some of Mercedes' production cars, but even now some of them—such as steer-by-wire—are still outlawed. With the car already more than a decade old, that's how farsighted the F400 was; it's still waiting for the rest of the world to catch up.

Above: This picture shows just how short the F400 was; there was hardly anything behind the two seats, which were placed well back in the car.

Left to right: For a company as conservative as Mercedes, the F400 was ridiculously wacky—it looked insane from every angle.

Technology

Mercedes didn't hold back when it came to packing the F400 with technology; just about every aspect of it was a break from the norm. Indeed, Mercedes referred to it as a mobile research laboratory, and while some of its features were too impractical to ever be used in a production car, there were plenty of real-world technologies in there, too.

For example, the fiber-optic headlights were more compact but much brighter than conventional units. The carbon ceramic brakes were also far more efficient and longer lasting than their more usual steel equivalent—if also vastly more costly.

However, it was the radical suspension design that was the key to the F400. The F400 featured computer-controlled adjustable suspension that allowed the wheels to lean by up to 20 degrees from the vertical. When combined with newly developed tires, there was up to 30 percent more lateral stability compared with a conventional system—a major benefit for safety. Those tires not only incorporated an asymmetrical tread pattern, but there were two of them per wheel. On the outside was a 19-inch (483-millimeter) tire for when the F400 was being driven in a straight line, while on the inside of the wheel there was a 17-inch (432-millimeter) tire for when the car was being cornered.

Other technologies packed into the F400 included an electrohydraulic braking system, electronic stability program, a by-wire electric steering system (with no mechanical linkages), and a 42-volt electrical system. Few of these would be used in production cars, unfortunately, but who knows what's around the corner?

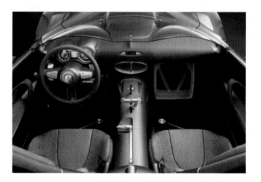

Top: The interior wasn't as out-there as the exterior, but it still looked neat.

Middle: Power was provided by Mercedes' familiar 3.2-liter straight-six.

Bottom: There was no weather protection provided of any kind; this was definitely a car for sunny climes.

Design

You don't have to study the F400 Carving for very long to see that its styling was, er, unconventional—to say the least. This should not be surprising, because the F400's designers found it extremely tricky coming up with an appealing exterior design when such a radical chassis technology had to be accommodated. They had to come up with a concept that allowed the wheels enough room to move during cornering with active camber control on the one hand, while also ensuring that the car looked good with the wheels in the normal position. Whether or not they succeeded on the "looking good" part is up to you.

Taking these criteria as the starting point, Mercedes launched a competition inviting young designers from the the company's studios in Germany, Japan, and the United States to come up with ideas. A flood of suggestions came in, ranging from utopian supercars to comical fun cruisers and from four-seater cabriolets to pure driving machines with one-man cockpits. Keeping in mind what won, it would be fascinating to see some of the designs that didn't make the grade.

The F400 was intended to evoke thoughts of a perfectly proportioned and superbly conditioned athlete: lean, muscular, and aggressive. From some angles, it also looked a little lopsided, and even more so once the doors were opened; they rose up sharp in a nod to the legendary 300SL Gull wing, launched exactly half a century before the F400.

Inside it was a minimalist fest, with little more than the bare essentials. There wasn't even a proper windshield; instead there was an aeroscreen. A pair of dials in front of the driver was just about all the instrumentation offered, but while it was pretty stripped-down, it reeked of quality, thanks to the alloy details that abounded. If there was one thing that really signaled the F400's intent, it was the four-point race harnesses fitted to each of the two seats.

At a Glance

Country of Manufacture
Germany

Engine
Front-mounted, normally aspirated V6

Displacement	195 ci (3,199 cc)
Power	221 bhp
Torque	232 lb.-ft.

Drivetrain
Six-speed sequential manual transmission, rear-wheel drive

Suspension, Wheels, and Brakes
Tires (inner): 255/45 R17

Tires (outer): 255/35 R19

Front brakes: 13-in. (330-mm) ventilated discs

Rear brakes: 13-in. (330-mm) ventilated discs

Weights and Measurements

Wheelbase	96 in. (2,450 mm)
Length	157 in. (3,979 mm)
Width	74 in. (1,890 mm)
Height	45 in. (1,150 mm)

Performance

0–62 mph	6.9 seconds
Top speed	150 mph (241 km/h)
Debut:	Paris 2001

Mini Rocketman (2011)

When BMW introduced an all-new Mini in 2001, it stirred up a storm. The original Mini of 1959 was a genuinely small car, wonderfully packaged and amazingly efficient. However, the new Mini was none of these things; it was big and—in the eyes of many—bloated, and, as a result, it was undeserving of the Mini tag. Indeed, there were some who felt it should have been called Maxi instead. However, keeping in mind the appalling reputation of the 1970s Austin of the same name, BMW naming its new not-so-small car the Maxi would have been seen as something of a marketing faux pas.

As it was, BMW churned out hundreds of thousands of copies of its new Mini before introducing an all-new model in 2006 that looked just like its predecessor. It was just as big and just as unimpressive with its interior packaging, although buyers still couldn't get enough thanks to great build quality, brilliant dynamics, and a rock-solid image.

What was really needed was a genuinely small Mini once again. During the decade that passed between BMW's introduction of the original Mini and the arrival of the Rocketman concept, the automotive landscape had changed immeasurably; a whole army of pretenders to the throne had appeared, threatening the Mini's dominance. What was needed was a genuinely small Mini that still offered a premium driving experience, safety, and style—and that's exactly what the Rocketman intended to provide.

The most obvious feature of the Rocketman was its diminutive proportions. At just 11-feet (3.4-meters) long, it was a mere 16 inches (400 millimeters) longer than the original Mini, which offered none of the crash protection or refinement of the newer car. The Rocketman also featured a far more high-tech construction, because its basis was a carbon-fiber unibody that was exposed between each door and front wheel. By using carbon fiber, the car's weight could be kept down while retaining strength. However, it would be a very costly way of making a car for the masses, so there was no way it could ever make production in such a form.

Above: It was immediately obvious that the Rocketman was a Mini, but no car ever made by BMW ever looked this funky.

Left to right: This twenty-first-century Mini was barely any bigger than the original, yet it was built to modern comfort and crash-safety standards.

Technology

BMW unveiled the Rocketman to shout about its design features, much more than its technological ones. That was a shame because this was a concept that was just crying out for a cutting-edge power train utilizing hybrid or electric power, or a latest-generation diesel engine. While Mini had embraced electric power for its production model, with the well-received Mini E, such technology was still seen as only for a small part of the market. What was more likely to power the Rocketman was a high-tech three-cylinder turbodiesel engine that offered performance with economy.

What was never in doubt was that the power would be sent to the front wheels; such a small car was reliant on the tightest possible packaging to free up the maximum amount of cabin space. However, if BMW opted for a gasoline/electric hybrid power train, it's possible that the engine may have powered the front wheels while an electric motor (or possibly one per wheel) would feed the power to the back to give a part-time four-wheel drive transmission.

While BMW kept quiet about the Rocketman's motive power, it was happy to reveal details of an array of new control systems that made the driver's life easier. These included a trackball on the multifunction steering wheel, which allowed drivers to control the car's major functions without having to move their hands to the center console. It was all cool, but no mention was made of what happened when the passenger wanted to adjust the settings . . .

Top: The double-hinged doors enabled easier access to the Rocketman's cabin, but they were also madly expensive for such a small car.

Middle: While the standard production Mini featured a distnctly retro interior, the Rocketman's cabin was more futuristic—and all the better for it.

Bottom: A neat touch was the slide-out drawer below the tailgate. It allowed bulkier items to be carried, just like with the original Mini.

Design

While the Rocketman's exterior design referenced the production BMW Mini more than the Issigonis original, the faux exposed door hinges came straight from the 1959 masterpiece. It was all new after that, especially the complex doors that were double-hinged so they opened away from the body shell, taking sections of the sill with them for easier entry and exit.

Such an expensive solution would never see the light of day and neither would the hooped LED rear lights, which looked superb if a little fragile. However, the front lights, which also incorporated LED technology, were destined to become a part of the third-generation production Mini.

The Rocketman's cabin was also seriously snazzy. This was partly because of the seat and dash design, but also because there was so much glass in evidence. Not only were the various pillars all very slender, but there was also a glass roof, etched with the Union Jack (the British flag) for an added dash of patriotism. The cabin was compact (perhaps a little too much for comfort), but it appeared bigger than it really was.

While the original Mini could seat four (or even five) in relative comfort, the Rocketman was really just a three seater (although a fourth person could be squeezed in if the journey wasn't too long and the extra passenger wasn't very big).

For a little extra practicality, there was a top-hinged tailgate, but unlike most hatchbacks, it ended at the base of the window. Below this there was a drawer instead of a conventional load bay, and for carrying bulky items, the drawer could be left out while the car was driven—something that was a direct reference to the original Mini's bottom-hinged trunk lid that could be left down for driving, thanks to its hinged license plate.

At a Glance

Country of Manufacture
UK/Germany

Engine
Front-mounted, probably a three-cylinder turbodiesel

Drivetrain
Probably a semiautomatic or sequential manual transmission with front-wheel drive

Suspension, Wheels, and Brakes
Wheels: 18 in. (457 mm) front and rear

Weights and Measurements

Length	135 in. (3,419 mm)
Width	75 in. (1,907 mm)
Height	55 in. (1,398 mm)

Performance
Fuel consumption 94 mpg

Debut:	Geneva 2011
Design director:	Anders Warming

Nissan Esflow (2011)

When the Nissan Esflow was unveiled in 2011, carmakers that offered little more than mediocrity on wheels were overlooked by many new car buyers. By this point in the evolution of cars, the stakes were too high to offer little more than the bare minimum. Consumers ruled, and they demanded cars that were safe, well built, well equipped, good to drive, and ecologically aware. They also wanted cars that looked great, too—cars that didn't look like all the others on the road.

When it comes to distinctive design, Nissan has had the guts to put more eye-catching cars into production than anyone else. Cars such as the Murano, Cube, 370Z, and Juke are unmistakable in their design, while the Leaf blazed a trail for electric cars, thanks to its clean-sheet design and excellent packaging. So when the Esflow was unveiled, Nissan had a pretty good track record for not insisting on following the crowd.

Nissan also had a great track record for producing wonderful drivers' cars; its Z cars of the 1970s are all-time greats, while the 200SX/Silvia that came in the 1980s and 1990s were also superb dynamically while remaining affordable. After a long period in the doldrums, Nissan revisited its Z car formula in 2003 with the introduction of the 350Z, which would go on to sire the even more highly regarded 370Z in 2008.

So the scene was set for something that looked great, that was wonderful to drive, and that was also far reaching technologically—and Esflow was all of those things. It was an eco-friendly rear-wheel-drive sports car powered purely by electricity; there was no internal combustion at all. The key thing about the Esflow was that it used available technology throughout. Indeed, because the Esflow used the same running gear as the Leaf production car, this sinewy concept could easily have been a sporty alternative to Nissan's electric-only family car. Whether or not there would have been enough buyers in such a fickle market sector was another matter—and clearly one that Nissan didn't want to have to contemplate.

Above: Nissan has never been afraid to embrace left-field design themes for its production cars, so the Esflow's lines were conservative in comparison.

Left to right: However you looked at it, there was no mistaking what the Esflow was all about. This was a sports car in the classic style.

Technology

Although to most people the idea of an electric car conjured up connotations of ugly toy cars crawling along at pedestrian speeds, there was nothing pedestrian about the Esflow. With only the rear wheels being driven—each one by its own electric motor—the Esflow promised an enticing dynamic balance.

These motors were powered by a laminated lithium-ion battery pack that was mounted low down in the chassis to keep the center of gravity very low. Because the Esflow was created as a pure-electric car from the outset, compromises didn't have to be made when it came to packaging the drivetrain—essential if the car's designers were to guarantee decent dynamics.

The battery packs were the same as those used in the Nissan Leaf, but in the Esflow they were located along the axis of the front and rear wheels to centralize the mass of the car, and thus its rotation point, close to the driver's hips.

It wasn't just about keeping the weight low down; by fitting the batteries in a line down the center of the car between the front and rear axles, the mass could be centralized, greatly improving the handling. The dynamics were further improved by the Esflow's lightweight construction; the body shell was made of carbon fiber, which was mounted on an aluminum chassis that incorporated its own roll cage. As a result, strength and lightness were offered, along with great agility—what was not to like?

Top: With its purely electric drivetrain, the Esflow's dash was expected to be high-tech—and that's exactly what it was, with its digital instrumentation.

Middle: Although the Esflow's controls were futuristic, many of the car's functions were still controlled via conventional means.

Bottom: Despite its complexity beneath the skin, the Esflow's cabin was surprisingly understated, with cream leather on most surfaces.

Opposite: Just take a moment to gaze at the futuristic flow and lines of the Esflow.

Design

With its oversize wheels and ridiculously short overhangs, the Esflow almost looked like a caricature of a car rather than an example of the real deal. It also looked surprisingly short, with the hood accounting for more of the car's length than you might expect—especially as there was no engine to house up front.

Most important, classic sports car design cues were in abundance: the steeply raked, wraparound windshield; the compact cabin placing the occupants right on the car's center of gravity; and hunched arches over ultralow profile tires wrapped around six-spoke wheels. You knew exactly who the Esflow was aimed at from the briefest of glances.

Naturally, there were design details galore aimed at optimizing the Esflow's aerodynamic efficiency. Door-mounted mirrors were replaced instead by rear-facing cameras at the base of the A-pillars to feed images to monitors inside the cabin. Meanwhile, charging points were incorporated into the air ducts built into the front end.

Saving weight was also a priority, which is why the cabin was an exercise in minimalism. Instead of bulky, thickly upholstered seats, the Esflow's seats were molded into its rear bulkhead. As a result, they were fixed, but because of the drive-by-wire technology, the pedals and steering wheel could easily be moved to find a comfortable driving position.

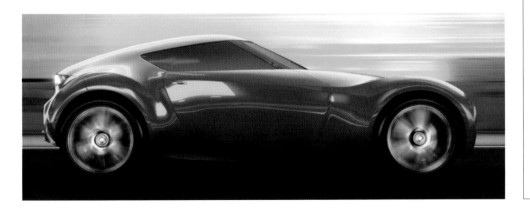

At a Glance

Country of Manufacture
Japan

Engine
Two electric motors, one for each rear wheel

Power supplied by lithium-ion battery pack, mounted centrally down the spine of the car

Power   214 bhp

Drivetrain
Rear-wheel drive

Performance
0–62 mph   Under 5 seconds

Range   150 miles (240 km)
                    approx.

Debut: Geneva 2011

Nissan Pivo 1 & 2 (2005/2007)

Pushing the boundaries is good, but sometimes you can't help thinking some people just don't know where to stop. That's exactly what anybody looking at the Nissan Pivo would have thought when it was unveiled in 2005. One of the most bizarre-looking machines ever unveiled at a motor show, the premise of the Pivo was completely insane; its entire passenger compartment could be turned through 360 degrees so the driver would never have to reverse.

The idea of the Pivo was that it offered greater maneuverability, visibility, and access than any car ever offered before. The fact that it was so unspeakably ugly as a result clearly counted against it, but sometimes when you think outside the box you end up with some pretty bizarre results. If there was one thing that the Pivo was, it was pretty bizarre.

So far removed from reality was the Pivo that it really did appear to have dropped in from another planet. In making something ludicrously overcomplex, Nissan's engineers took everyday items from the modern car and reengineered them, at what appeared to be maximum cost, to come up with a car that could never be economically viable. As if all this wasn't enough, Nissan created a sequel to the Pivo two years later, predictably called the Pivo 2 and still packing far too much technology.

Taking the original Pivo concept and looking no less crazy, the Pivo 2 incorporated a stack of new safety features to help prevent Pivo drivers from crashing into each other. These included distance control assist and around view monitor, both of which were intended to improve visibility for the driver. Keeping in mind the number of glazed surfaces already featured, one could only assume that Nissan was counting on a lot of partially sighted people buying the Pivo, which let's face it you'd probably have to be—nobody else would want to be seen in one of these creations. Sometimes it's good to dream, but if you're not careful such exercises can quickly turn into nightmares . . .

Above: Few carmakers can do off-the-wall like Nissan does; the Pivo was utterly crazy in terms of concept and execution, yet the company came up with an equally far-fetched sequel.

Left to right: This blue car is the sequel to the first model, as shown above. It was just as crazy as its predecessor, but incorporated more safety features.

Technology

It was easy to look at the Pivo and dismiss it as nothing more than a flight of fancy—something dreamed up by a designer who had probably been smoking something that he really shouldn't have. However, underneath that jaw-dropping exterior design was an array of technologies that might just have had some value, along with some that probably didn't.

Among those in the latter category was a piece of tech that let drivers motion toward a sensor for the car to automatically activate various controls—which was probably fine as long as they didn't sneeze at the wrong time.

Of more use was the drive-by-wire system, which freed up space in the cabin and improved safety by dispensing with all mechanical linkages. Another technology that was definitely of value, but at the time was unlikely to provide Nissan with riches beyond its wildest dreams, was the purely electric drivetrain. There was an electric motor for each axle, with power coming from a battery mounted in the center of the car. In time, Nissan would go on to build the world's first mainstream production electric car created from the outset as an electric vehicle. Unlike its rivals, the Leaf was no mere adaptation of an internal combustion-engined car, and thankfully it looked nothing like the Pivo.

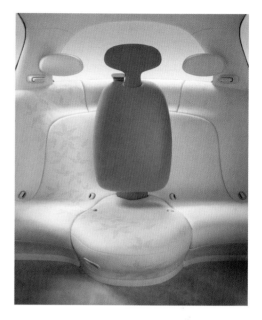

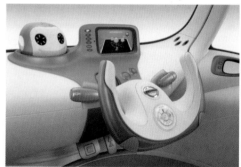

Top: There was a neat seating arrangement, with the driver sat in the middle, flanked by passengers on each side. This is the Pivo 2.

Middle: Everywhere you looked in the Pivos there were organic shapes and soft-touch materials in a bid to soothe the car's occupants.

Bottom: The Pivo 1 overcomplicated things by featuring a screen and camera for the front three-quarter view—instead of just having a quarterlight for better visibility.

Opposite: This variant color theme looks a little less toylike, but still bizarre.

Design

Being behind the wheel of a Pivo was as close as anyone would get to driving a goldfish bowl, which probably wouldn't suit most people, but it did ensure one thing: that all-around visibility wasn't much of an issue. With its vast expanses of glass and slender see-through pillars, the Pivo was as light and airy inside as possible.

Instead of conventional hinges for the doors, they opened out and back on parallelogram hinges, with electric assistance. It may have been a complicated arrangement, but it did make life easy for users while also providing the easiest entry and exit imaginable.

Once inside, the driver sat up front and in the middle, with the two passengers located to each side and slightly behind. The fully digital dash was in a strip along the base of the windshield, while the steering wheel (which wasn't really a wheel at all) incorporated much of the switch gear more usually seen scattered around the dashboard.

The exterior featured some pretty neat thinking, too, in terms of functionality, because it incorporated oval recesses into the front and rear. These were covered with soft materials, so there would always be somewhere comfortable to sit outside when the Pivo was parked.

At a Glance

Country of Manufacture
Japan

Engine
Front- and rear-mounted electric motors powered by a lithium-ion battery

Drivetrain
Automatic, four-wheel drive

Weights and Measurements
Curb weight	2,425 lb. (1,100 kg)
Wheelbase	79 in. (2,000 mm)
Length	106 in. (2,700 mm)
Width	63 in. (1,600 mm)

Performance
Top speed	60 mph (96 km/h)
Debut:	Tokyo 2005

Opel Flextreme (2007)

For years, General Motors had been complacent with its showroom products. The result of lazy design, the products of European divisions, such as Opel, Saab, and Vauxhall, had lost their individuality as well as their desirability. With conventionally engineered and predictable offerings, it was no surprise when General Motors went bankrupt little more than a year after the Opel Flextreme concept was revealed late in 2007.

However, the Flextreme showed that things could have been so different. When it was unveiled, it was the latest in a line of economy concepts, which started with the electrically powered Opel GT in 1971. In the meantime there had been the Tech 1 of 1981, the Impuls of 1990, and the Eco 2 that arrived a year later. There were a lot more along the way, the best known being the ultrastylish pure-electric EV1, which was only available for lease. Owners loved their EV1s, but GM didn't; they were all reclaimed and crushed.

Fast forward to 2007, and electric cars would soon be unveiled by mainstream carmakers as regular production vehicles. Such technology had its drawbacks, which is why the range extender was seen as a more viable alternative; in these, the car's batteries are kept charged by an onboard internal combustion engine. While Opel claimed its Flextreme could be powered by a hydrogen fuel cell, it chose to keep the concept more in the real world by fitting a conventional engine instead.

So with the Flextreme, a commuter living within 30 miles (48 kilometers) of their workplace, and, therefore, with a round-trip commute of 60 miles (96 kilometers) each day, would need no diesel fuel and, therefore, emit zero CO_2. They would just need to charge up their car each evening and during work. Even if the owner forgot to recharge, or had to undertake a longer journey, the Flextreme remained clean and economical because it would emit less than 40 grams per kilometer (about two-thirds of a mile) CO_2 in combustion mode. So whichever way you look at it, the Flextreme was capable of out-greening any production car available at the time.

Above: For years, Opels had featured styling that was nondescript to say the least, but not here; the Flextreme looked superb.

Left to right: Opel would have liked to fit a fuel cell to the Flextreme, but decided to keep things more real-world by opting for a gasoline/electric hybrid system.

Technology

Around the time that the Flextreme was unveiled, there was an oversupply of hybrid concept and production cars being released by carmakers around the globe—and this was a decade after the first production models had gone on sale. Without exception, they were all cars that were driven by an internal combustion engine, which was assisted by an electric motor—powered by battery pack.

The Flextreme turned this on its head. The wheels were always driven by an electric motor, which was powered by a battery that was kept topped up by a 1.3-liter turbodiesel engine. So the engine was there purely to act as a generator to keep the lithium-ion batteries recharged.

The problem with purely electric cars is that battery technology can't provide a range anywhere near that of an internal combustion engine, so there's always the chance of being stranded on a reasonably long journey. However, most journeys are relatively short and an electric car would be fine for the job much of the time. To counter the "range anxiety" inherent when undertaking a longer journey, an onboard generator, to keep the batteries topped up, is the perfect solution.

Reducing the Flextreme'e weight as much as possible was key to maximizing its efficiency, which is why there were lightweight body panels along with polycarbonate glazing. By taking this route, these elements were 40 percent lighter than usual, while the plastic panels also helped to provide better pedestrian safety.

Top: The cabin was ultramodern, and featured neutral colors for a feeling of extra space. A glass roof made it feel even more airy.

Middle: Access to the trunk was via two gull-wing doors, which looked intriguing but didn't really add much in the way of practicality.

Bottom: Predictably, there was no analog instrumentation at all, with all information conveyed via digital displays.

Design

The Flextreme was all about offering real-world efficiency, which meant that although it had to be superfrugal, this couldn't be at the expense of usability. As a result, the cabin had to be able to seat real people—and adults at that—while there also had to be a usable load bay. So while the Flextreme looked farsighted, its basic packaging meant it wasn't as far in the future as it appeared.

The Flextreme's basic shape was a monobox, so from the short front end to the upright tail there was a single continuous arc. Offering excellent aerodynamics with top-notch packaging, this single-box shape was also packed with cool details for even greater efficiency.

For example, the air intakes were far smaller than usual, thanks to the much-reduced cooling requirements for the range extender power train. A neat touch is the transparent trim that was used to enclose the front end-mounted badging as well as the sharply styled alloy wheels. By enclosing such details, but without making it obvious, the car's aerodynamic efficiency could be much improved without the need to make it look bland.

Fully open, the Flextreme looked like it was ready to take flight.

At a Glance

Country of Manufacture
Germany

Engine
Front-mounted, turbodiesel four-cylinder

Displacement	76 ci (1,248 cc)
Power	161 bhp
Torque	273 lb.-ft.

Drivetrain
Single electric motor powered by lithium-ion batteries, front-wheel drive

Suspension, Wheels, and Brakes
Front suspension: Independent, with MacPherson struts

Rear suspension: Torsion beam

Wheel diameter: 21 in. (533 mm)

Front tires: 195/45 R21

Rear tires: 195/45 R21

Weights and Measurements

Wheelbase	107 in. (2,725 mm)
Length	179 in. (4,555 mm)
Width	72 in. (1,836 mm)
Height	59 in. (1,487 mm)
Turning circle	35 ft. 9 in. (10.9 m)

Performance

0–62 mph	9.5 seconds
Top speed	100 mph (161 km/h)
Range	445 miles (716 km)
Electric-only range	34 miles (55 km)
CO_2 emissions	40 g/km

Debut:	Frankfurt 2007
Design director:	Anthony Lo

Peugeot Hoggar (2003)

If concept cars are about escapism, the Peugeot Hoggar must rate as one of the greatest concepts of all time. Sure, it didn't look that futuristic, but this was one of those cars that fell into the category of not standing even the remotest chance of being built by Peugeot. However, there was nothing so far-reaching about its design, technology, or construction that precluded it from being built at all, so what a shame that a specialty carmaker wasn't prepared to offer the Hoggar as a low-volume special.

The premise of the Hoggar was to offer go-anywhere fun while also retaining a social conscience—if you can successfully claim that any car packing two engines really has a social conscience. Having two power plants was for those scenarios when too much power is not enough; with the throttle pressed to the metal, the two engines would each catapult the car forward and keep it accelerating swiftly to its undisclosed top speed. However, in normal driving, when relatively little power was required, just one engine would be used. It was in this mode that it could be argued that the Hoggar had some kind of social conscience, although just looking at the thing it's doubtful that you'd get anyone else to agree.

Incidentally, the Hoggar took its name from a desert in Algeria, so bonus points if you spotted that; few people did. Knowing that, it's easier to see just where Peugeot was pitching this boundary-pushing 4x4, not that the briefest of glances was likely to leave you in any doubt. Looking like the kind of thing you'd expect to see bouncing over the dunes in some ultrahot part of the world, the Hoggar was just the type of vehicle that Peugeot should have created for an entry into the Paris-Dakar rally. Unfortunately, it never did, but had it done so, it would have shaken things up.

Above: A four-cylinder diesel engine might not sound like a recipe for excitement, but when you've got one at each end, things start to get more interesting.

Left to right: Just the briefest of glances indicated what the Hoggar was built for; traversing tricky off-road terrain in hot climates.

Technology

The Hoggar didn't look especially futuristic, but some of the technology it incorporated was cutting edge for production cars. The drivetrain consisted of a pair of Peugeot's tried-and-tested 2.2-liter HDi turbodiesel engines, one mounted at the front and the other at the back.

At this time, diesel engines were gaining in popularity thanks to them being inherently more efficient than equivalent gasoline units. Much more refined than they'd ever been before, the torquey nature of a turbodiesel engine was also perfectly suited to a 4x4 like the Hoggar, but until now such power plants had also been inherently dirtier than an equivalent gasoline unit, thanks to the particulates produced.

Peugeot was a pioneer in the particulate filter, which cleaned up a diesel-engine car's exhaust emissions enormously, and it was this technology that the Hoggar showcased. As a result, the Hoggar packed a huge 590 lb.-ft. of torque, yet its emissions were relatively small—not that any official figure was disclosed.

Each engine had its own six-speed transmission, but because each one was controlled electronically, it wasn't as though the driver had to wrestle with a pair of gear shift sticks. The driver could leave the transmissions to do their own thing by leaving the system in fully automatic mode, or there was a sequential manual option, with ratios being selected by paddle shifts on the steering wheel.

Top: Simplicity was the key word to describe the Hoggar's interior, but it still featured luxurious materials, such as leather and aluminum, for that natural look.

Middle: There was no weather protection of any kind, but there was a strong roll cage in case the driver parked the Hoggar on its roof.

Bottom: For such a brute of a car, many of the details were surprisingly delicate—and they worked all the better for it.

Opposite: This sketch shows the Hoggar at its most comfortable—with a racing driver at the wheel.

Design

Short overhangs had become fashionable around the time the Hoggar was unveiled, but this was a car that took such a look to extremes; the wheels couldn't have been placed any farther apart. Indeed, at the back of the Hoggar, the wheels were almost proud of the bodywork, while the only thing ahead of the front wheels was a grille—you'd search in vain for bumpers at either end of the car.

What dominated the Hoggar's design was the exposed mechanicals. On show was the front and rear suspension, while the side exhausts would have been a health and safety inspector's nightmare. At least the engine wasn't left exposed, although keeping it on display behind a glass panel would have spiced things up visually even more.

The idea behind the Hoggar's overall design was that it looked like an animal, ready to pounce. The front wing line flowed right through to the rear haunches of the car, while the slitted headlights were meant to evoke the look of a cat keeping watch. Whether or not this inspiration was obvious is open to debate, but there's no denying that despite the aggressive, functional look of the Hoggar, it also came across as a surprisingly cohesive design.

At a Glance

Country of Manufacture
France

Engine
Front and rear-mounted, four-cylinder turbodiesel

Displacement	132 ci (2,168 cc) x 2
Power	221 bhp x 2
Torque	295 lb.-ft. x 2

Drivetrain
Six-speed sequential manual transmission, four-wheel drive

Suspension, Wheels, and Brakes
Front suspension: Double wishbones, twin coil springs and shock absorbers, antiroll bar

Rear suspension: Double wishbones, twin coil springs and shock absorbers, antiroll bar

Front brakes: 15-in. (380-mm) ventilated discs with six piston calipers

Rear brakes: 15-in. (380-mm) ventilated discs with six piston calipers

Wheels: 21-in. (533-mm) alloy wheels with Michelin tires, front and rear

Weights and Measurements

Curb weight	2,866 lb. (1,300 kg)
Wheelbase	108 in. (2,750 mm)
Length	156 in. (3,960 mm)
Width	79 in. (2,000 mm)
Height	59 in. (1,490 mm)
Debut:	Geneva 2003

Peugeot BB1 (2009)

Over the years, Peugeot has built some pretty farsighted concept cars, not least of all its Oxia, Proxima, and Quasar concepts of the 1980s. Unabashed supercars that would never see the light of day in any form, such cars showed what was possible but far from likely. This wasn't meant to be the case with the BB1, which was at the opposite end of the motoring spectrum, because it was a tiny car designed to carry people using as little space and as few resources as possible. As a result, it summed up its era when it was released in 2009.

With the global economy in meltdown, energy prices threatening to bankrupt many, and ecology a recurring theme worldwide, regardless of industry, the BB1 was perfectly timed. Tiny and powered solely by electricity, the BB1 was cheap to run, maneuverable, and frugal, while also looking impossibly funky. Unusually, it was also reasonably real-world worthy in that the technologies it showcased were all available when the car was unveiled in 2009. Whether or not the BB1 could be built economically—and whether or not there would be enough buyers for such a quirky car—were another matter entirely.

The key thing was that Peugeot accepted mobility as a key facet of modern life; trying to legislate or price people off the road was simply not going to work. The answer lay in creating smaller, more efficient cars so that personal transportation was still an option for the masses. The BB1 would consume the minimum of the world's resources while also taking up as little road space as possible. To do this, Peugeot set its design team a seemingly impossible brief: to create a car just 8 feet 2½ inches (2.5 meters) long, capable of seating four adults—and they did it.

Above: With proportions like these, it would be easy to assume that the BB1 was merely a two seater, but it could actually seat four.

Left to right: The sharply rising waistline gave the BB1 more dynamism, and while the overall shape was neat, that bulbous windshield didn't really work aesthetically.

Technology

The key thing that distanced the BB1 from mainstream production cars of the time was its motive power; this was a purely electric city car. It was much quieter than conventionally powered cars and cleaner, too, if it could be powered from renewable energies.

Each rear wheel was driven by a 10 brake horsepower electric motor, fed energy by a lithium-ion battery pack, which offered a claimed range of up to 75 miles (120 kilometers). Despite this seemingly puny power output—and thanks to a prodigious amount of torque—the BB1 was much more sprightly than it sounded; it could get from 0 to 20 miles (32 kilometers) per hour in just 2.8 seconds. Acceleration around town was also pretty strong, but it was the BB1's handling that should have impressed, because the running gear was located low down in the car, reducing the center of gravity. The overall weight was kept down, too, by building the BB1's body shell from ultralight carbon fiber; the result was a car that tipped the scales at just 1,323 pounds (600 kilograms), even with the battery pack fitted.

To fit four people into such a tiny cabin, space had to be found in whichever way possible. One innovative way of doing this was to ditch key functions, such as a GPS system, telephone, radio, and MP3 player, by hooking the car up to the owner's smartphone. In this way, the dash could be kept free of clutter, although accessing multiple functions on the move may have proved more of a challenge than it should have been.

Top: The use of rear-hinged doors helped the two back-seat passengers to climb aboard. It was a very neat solution.

Middle: By using a motorcycle style of seating arrangement, it was possible to accommodate four adults more easily.

Bottom: In keeping with the motorcycle theme, there was a set of handlebars instead of a steering wheel; the glass roof opened up the cabin even more.

Design

Take a look at pretty much any car you like—whether it's a concept or production model—and it'll have that swept-back look. The lines will be moving from the front toward the rear, whether that's the windshield, the waistline, or the rear deck. As a result, the car will have added dynamism; it'll look as though it's moving even when it's standing still. That's usually the Holy Grail of car designers, but not with the BB1; its windshield was upright and the A-pillars were swept forward instead of back. Indeed, at first glance it would almost have been easy to think it was being driven backward if it weren't for the rear lights being so prominent.

The inspiration for the BB1's design and packaging came from motorcycles. It was intended to be much more than simply a four-wheeled motorcycle, and the thinking was good because, by seating the rear passengers in the same way that an extra person would sit on a motorcycle, it was possible to seat four adults in a car that was just 8 feet 2½ inches (2.5 meters) long. Well, in theory, anyway . . . If you're not impressed by that, keep in mind that an original Mini was just over 9 feet 9½ inches (3 meters) long, while a second-generation Smart ForTwo is 8 feet 9½ inches (2.7 meters) long, yet it can seat only two.

To fit everyone in, the structure of the passenger compartment aped the classic motorcycle design: the driver controlled the BB1 by adopting a more vertical driving position than usual, made possible through the absence of floor pedals. The rear passengers were seated in tandem behind the driver.

Access to the BB1 was through an inverted door-opening mechanism, while trunk access was through a tailboard and a tailgate. So while the BB1's exterior design was certainly challenging, it was also one of the most innovatively resolved concepts of its time.

At a Glance

Country of Manufacture
France

Engine
Twin rear-mounted electric motors

Continuous power	20 bhp
Peak power	27 bhp
Torque	472 lb.-ft.

Drivetrain
Rear-wheel drive

Suspension, Wheels, and Brakes
Michelin Energy Saver tires all around

Front tires: 195/50 R16

Rear tires: 195/50 R16

Weights and Measurements

Curb weight	1,323 lb. (600 kg)
Wheelbase	71 in. (1,800 mm)
Length	98 in. (2,500 mm)
Width	63 in. (1,600 mm)
Drag coefficient	0.36
Turning circle	11 ft. (3.5 m)

Performance

0–20 mph	2.8 seconds
Top speed	56 mph (90 km/h)
Range	75 miles (120 km)
Debut:	Frankfurt 2009

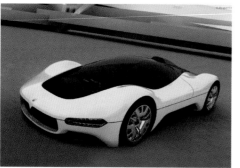

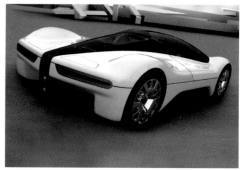

Pininfarina Birdcage 75th (2005)

Pininfarina has a history of creating jaw-dropping concepts. The Ferrari Dino Berlinetta Speciale of 1965 was the first to be based on then cutting-edge racing car mechanicals; it was followed in 1967 by the Dino Competizione. However, most amazing of all was the Modulo of 1970, which appeared to consist of a single curve above four enclosed wheels— a seminal supercar that arguably lent more to the Birdcage 75th than any of Pininfarina's previous dream cars.

While all these concepts used Ferraris as their basis, the first competition car-derived Pininfarina special was based on the Maserati A6 GCS of 1954. Maserati had a glorious heritage, but it was always the poor relation to Ferrari. So, to celebrate Pininfarina's seventy-fifth birthday, the design house decided to do an update of a Maserati milestone: the legendary Tipo 61, or "Birdcage," of 1959.

The result was a Birdcage for the twenty-first century, except that Pininfarina didn't exactly overdose on the retro design themes, despite the name. For starters, the original Birdcage was purely a racing car; there was never any road-going version offered. Also, while the original was an open car, the new one was closed. Most unusually of all, despite taking that hallowed Birdcage name, few styling cues were taken from the 1959 car. Indeed, aside from the heavily pronounced wheel arches, there was little to link the new car, visually, to the old.

None of this really mattered, of course. What really mattered was that the Birdcage 75th was a dream car of the highest order. It was impractical, featured incredible styling, and was powered by a fabulous engine. It was also completely unsuited to production, just like all the best concept cars.

Above: Pininfarina has been responsible for some of the most adventurous supercar designs ever created, so the Birdcage was a fitting seventy-fifth birthday tribute.

Left to right: The Birdcage was definitely about show rather than practicality, but it was also a fully driveable prototype.

Technology

The Birdcage 75th had to be an ultimate—something that would stop the Geneva Motor Show when it was unveiled. That meant some pretty radical mechanicals, so what better than those that normally lived under the ultraexclusive Maserati MC12, itself based on the Ferrari Enzo? Using this platform meant the car had a 6-liter V12, placed in the middle for the best possible weight distribution. This sent its power to the rear wheels courtesy of a six-speed sequential manual transmission that allowed lightning-fast gear changes for maximum acceleration.

More interestingly were the high-tech information and communication systems integrated within the Birdcage 75th's cabin. Developed by Motorola, the technology carried the tag "seamless mobility." Its purpose was to allow users to access information on the move, while also communicating with friends and family. There was a built-in phone, wireless Internet, text pager, and a two-way radio. The cabin of the Birdcage 75th wasn't the place to be if you wanted to remain incommunicado.

With 700 brake horsepower to rein in, the Birdcage had to be fitted with some powerful brakes, and sure enough there was a Brembo system installed that was comprised of drilled and ventilated discs at each corner. Measuring a monstrous 15 inches (380 millimeters) across up front and 13 inches (335 millimeters) at the rear, there were also alloy callipers that featured six pistons at the front and four at the back. To help get the power down there was an equally impressive suspension system; using race car technology, there were pushrods at each end along with single-calibrated shock absorbers and coaxial coil springs.

Top: A head-up display was one of the key features of the Birdcage's interior; it was effectively a virtual dashboard at the base of the windshield.

Middle: The seriously low roof line meant a semi-reclining driving position had to be adopted, for both of the Birdcage's occupants.

Bottom: Instead of conventional instruments, everything was projected in the Birdcage's interior, onto the windshield and steering wheel.

Design

The Birdcage 75th was—to a degree—more about form than function. However, there is a theory that says that the two are inextricably linked, and that could certainly be argued in this case. That's because while the Birdcage 75th's design was based around aerodynamic and packaging efficiency, it also had to offer a degree of usability—even if not that much.

Pininfarina started by taking the Maserati MC12's rolling chassis and working out how it could be clothed as tightly as possible. That meant as low a roofline as practicable, while using teardrop and inverted fender forms for high-speed stability with minimal drag. The end result was a car that sat little more than 3 feet (1 meter) off the ground—something that was accentuated even more by the enormous wheels, which measured 20 inches (508 millimeters) in diameter at the front and 22 inches (559 millimeters) at the back.

To aid high-speed stability, the whole of the back of the car was dominated by an enormous diffuser, while there were also adjustable fins in the sills. To help reduce the height of the car front and rear, LED lighting was used—something that was far more compact than conventional halogen illumination.

It was arguably from above that the Birdcage 75th looked the most impressive, because glass ran for virtually the whole of the car's length. At the front this constituted the canopy, while at the rear it helped to showcase the magnificent V12.

If the Birdcage 75th's exterior looked amazing, the cabin was no less jaw dropping with its futuristic design and luxurious Alcantara finish. A head-up display was the centerpiece, which was effectively a virtual dashboard projected below the windshield. The key information usually displayed in dial form on the dash was instead produced in digital form on the steering wheel, which in 1959 would have seemed like something from another planet.

At a Glance

Country of Manufacture
Italy

Engine
Midmounted, normally aspirated gas V12

Displacement	366 ci (5,998 cc)
Power	700 bhp

Drivetrain
Six-speed sequential manual transmission, rear-wheel drive

Suspension, Wheels, and Brakes
Front suspension: Pushrod with double wishbones, coil springs, and shock absorbers

Rear suspension: Pushrod with double wishbones, coil springs, and shock absorbers

Front brakes: 15-in. (380-mm) ventilated discs with six-piston calipers

Rear brakes: 13-in. (335-mm) ventilated discs with four-piston calipers

Front tires: 275/30 R20

Rear tires: 295/35 R22

Weights and Measurements

Curb weight	3,307 lb. (1,500 kg)
Wheelbase	110 in. (2,800 mm)
Length	183 in. (4,656 mm)
Width	80 in. (2,020 mm)
Height	43 in. (1,090 mm)
Debut:	Geneva 2005

Renault DeZir (2010)

Renault was on something of a roll with its concept cars around the time that the DeZir was unveiled. Unfortunately for the company, things weren't looking so rosy for its production cars; they featured unadventurous styling and conventional engineering, and the company had a lackluster image. Despite a raft of image-building concepts, such as the Captur, Frendzy, and DeZir, there was little sign of the company's showroom offerings becoming any more distinctive. It was no wonder Renault's sales were on the slide; if only it had the courage to make its production cars more eye-catching.

Distinctive design was something not lacking in the DeZir, which was built for a segment in which Renault had never really competed: the compact GT. The closest Renault had ever got to this niche before was the Sport Spider, although that was an open car. However, collaborations with Alpine right up until the 1990s had seen cars in this segment wearing Renault badges, so the positioning of the DeZir wasn't entirely without precedent.

What made the DeZir intriguing was its purely electric drivetrain; for a sporting coupé, that was a novel diversion from the norm. However, while Renault wasn't afraid to put smaller, more practical electric cars into production, such as the Twizy and Zoe, it wasn't going to risk offering an electric sporting coupé. It had already had its fingers burned with the bizarre Avantime and Vel Satis, which had been costly to develop, but nobody wanted to buy. So it's a shame that the DeZir never reached production, because there were probably a lot of people who would have bought one just to put it in their garage and look at it, even if they never took it out.

Above: Renault's design had been in the doldrums for years; however, the DeZir showed that the company was capable of producing great-looking cars.

Left to right: While the door design was needlessly wacky, the rest of the DeZir worked wonderfully, so it's a shame that Renault never built it.

Technology

Perhaps the key thing about the DeZir technologically was that it featured purely electric drive, and even more important, the components for this were taken pretty much wholesale from Renault's production electric cars. So it was tried-and-tested stuff, not just pie-in-the-sky thinking that would probably never be realized.

Motive power came from a motor that was mounted in a midrear position, which was fed electricity from a lithium-ion battery fitted behind the bench seat. Offering a range of 100 miles (160 kilometers), the battery pack could be charged in just 20 minutes if the correct 400-volt three-phase supply was available. Otherwise it was a question of leaving it charging for 8 hours from a conventional power outlet—although an exchange battery scheme, as proposed by Renault, would speed things up even more.

To help keep the batteries charged on the move, the car employed a regenerative braking system, and great attention was paid to efficiency to increase the range as much as possible. As a result, not only was the car very aerodynamically efficient (it had a drag coefficient of just 0.25), but it was also very light. A curb weight of just 1,830 pounds (830 kilograms) was very impressive for an electric car, with the weight being reduced to the max thanks to the extensive use of lightweight materials, such as Kevlar.

Top: As was becoming increasingly common at the time, the DeZir's interior looked as though it had melted; it was supposed to be an organic look.

Middle: It was Laurens van den Acker who oversaw the DeZir's design; he'd previously worked for Audi, Ford, and Mazda.

Bottom: Those doors were weird just for the sake of it; there was no real reason for having them hinged at opposing ends.

Opposite: The side view, in particular, showcases the just slightly ridiculous size of the DeZir's wheels.

Design

The first car to be overseen by Renault's then-new design director Laurens van den Acker, the DeZir was also the first model to show the company's new design language. While the design language didn't actually have a name, it did have a philosophy—namely that any car featuring it should be simple, sensuous, and warm. Whether or not the DeZir achieved that is up to you, but most who saw it reckoned it managed at least two of the three, if not the full hat trick.

The thing that struck you first about the DeZir was its amazing compound curves; it was wonderfully curvaceous from every angle. Lead designer Yann Jarsalle explained: "My early source of inspiration stemmed from the liquid sensation, wavelike movement, and contrasts in light associated with certain rippled surfaces"—which is why you'll search in vain for any evidence of a straight line.

Like all the best concepts, the wheels were just a bit too large to be truly practical; in the case of the DeZir, they were 21 inches (533 millimeters) across, which is why the fenders were so heavily sculpted to accommodate them. Meanwhile, the sides featured a combination of flush and recessed forms that played on contrasting light patterns, which really made the most of that superb red paintwork.

Most important, the DeZir's front-end design previewed the new front-end identity that was poised to become a feature of all Renault's production cars from that point on. Unfortunately, none of them had the presence of this fabulous emissions-free coupé.

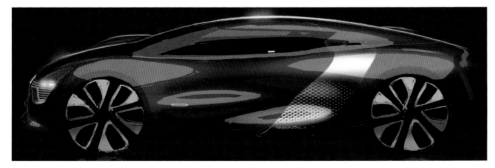

At a Glance

Country of Manufacture
France

Engine
Midmounted electric motor with 24 kWh lithium-ion battery

Power	150 bhp
Torque	167 lb.-ft.

Drivetrain
Electric drive, active differential, rear-wheel drive

Suspension, Wheels, and Brakes
245/35 R21 tires front and rear

14-in. (356-mm) ventilated discs front and rear

Weights and Measurements

Curb weight	1,830 lb. (830 kg)
Wheelbase	102 in. (2,582 mm)
Length	166 in. (4,225 mm)
Width	78 in. (1,986 mm)
Height	46 in. (1,163 mm)
Ground clearance	4 in. (110 mm)

Performance

0–62 mph	5 seconds
Top speed	112 mph (180 km/h)
Range	100 miles (160 km)

Debut:	Paris 2010
Design director:	Laurens van den Acker
Exterior designer:	Yann Jarsalle

Rinspeed Senso (2005)

Swiss eccentric Frank Rinderknecht set up Rinspeed in the late 1970s to import sunroofs from the United States, but it wasn't long before he was tuning BMWs, Porsches, and Volkswagens. By the 1980s, Rinspeed was creating some of the most outrageous machines around, especially some of his Porsches that mixed 911 body shells with 928 elements.

By the end of the twentieth century, Rinspeed had started to come up with the most out of this world concept cars anywhere. For years, Rinderknecht could be relied upon to produce something utterly crazy for the annual spring Geneva Motor Show. He did it all: SUVs on steroids, electric city cars, and subaqua sports cars—nothing was off Rinderknecht's radar. If somehow all this craziness passed you by, just Google the company's Exasis, Bedouin, Tattoo, or X-Trem, and you'll see this is no overstatement.

So when the Senso was unveiled at the 2005 Geneva Motor Show, it didn't seem quite as out there as it might have done; sure, it looked a bit odd, but we'd seen some far more bizarre creations emerge from the company's workshops. However, the technology packed within the Senso was nothing less than from another planet. Indeed, most who saw it just couldn't see the point; here was a car that monitored its driver's biometric data and adjusted various parameters to suit. As a result, its creator called this "the most sensuous car in the world"— something that Toyota may have taken issue with, thanks to the development of its Pod concept, which did much the same thing.

The Senso took into account the driver's pulse and driving behavior, then adjusted the music, interior lighting, and even the fragrances to suit. As a result, it could soothe a frustrated driver or pep up a tired one; however, Rinspeed didn't say what it could do for a driver who was both frustrated and tired.

Above: Rinspeed is no stranger to weird concepts, and while the Senso didn't look as odd as some of its previous efforts, its premise was just as strange.

Left to right: The Senso was definitely not a looker, which is a shame because beneath that bulky bodywork is a Porsche-sourced 3.2-liter flat 6.

Technology

Despite its 3.2-liter Porsche Boxster gasoline engine, the Senso claimed to be green because it ran on natural gas—although a lot of it, no doubt. This sent its power to the rear wheels via a six-speed manual transmission. Indeed, aside from the natural-gas element, the Senso was disappointingly conventional in its drivetrain.

One innovative touch was the suspension, which was infinitely adjustable in terms of its ride height and stiffness to provide the perfect ride/handling balance. The whole point of the Senso, however (if it could be argued that there was a point), was to sense its driver's biometric data and adjust a range of parameters accordingly.

Inputs were courtesy of an elaborate system that consisted of a number of sensors that gathered data about the driver's condition. A biometric Polar watch measured a driver's pulse while a mobile eye camera recorded driving behavior, such as how well and how often lanes were changed, along with how close and at what speed the Senso approached the cars in front. An onboard computer then evaluated the data to establish the driver's state of mind.

This, in turn, controlled four small liquid crystal displays (LCDs), which could emit stimulating (orange/yellow), relaxing (blue/violet), or neutral (green) color patterns into the driver's line of vision. As if this wasn't enough, various fragrances could be pumped into the car through the air vents for a calming or stimulating effect.

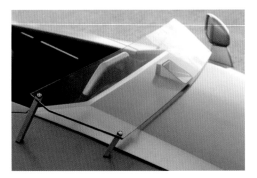

Top: This was the most flattering view of the Senso; from this angle the concept almost looked sleek—but not quite.

Middle: There were seats for three occupants inside: the driver sat up front on their own, flanked by passengers to each side, behind.

Bottom: In place of a conventional windshield, there was this aeroscreen-type affair, which looked more like a bathroom shelf.

Opposite: The Senso tried to cut a fine figure on the racetrack—and failed.

Design

Rinspeed has never worried too much about good looks or practicality, and nowhere was this more evident than with the Senso, which looked awkward from most angles and featured nothing in the way of protection from the elements.

Its exterior lines were inspired by industrial architecture; cue some PR hype: "It creates a tension-filled dynamic between moving and nonmoving objects. The two-part structure of the rear end is reminiscent of bold roof constructions and deep chasms between ranks of skyscrapers. The interplay between smooth curves and sharp edges evokes attractive industrial architecture." Yeah, whatever.

Rinspeed called this a no-nonsense look; those who criticized it could easily have claimed it was more of a no-effort look. At least the bodywork was created entirely from recylable composites. While the windshield was fashioned from polycarbonate, it was much lighter than a conventional glass item and was also scratch-proof.

The interior was just as unconventional, and it was also clearly inspired by industrial architecture too. In the center of the Senso was the driver, who sat up front in the middle; behind was a pair of seats, making this a three seater, just like the McLaren F1. Unfortunately for any would-be Senso buyers, that's just about the only thing this Rinspeed oddball had in common with the supercar great.

Saab PhoeniX (2011)

Saab didn't particularly need to unveil a concept at the 2011 Geneva Motor Show; the world's press was already focused on this once-great Swedish marque as it was on the verge of bankruptcy. However, now under new ownership, Saab reckoned that what it needed to do to celebrate a year of independence, having finally split from the huge General Motors conglomerate, was to unveil a statement—something to say that the company was in good health and that it was all set to enjoy a great new era of producing innovative cars.

Except, of course, Saab wasn't in good health; for months afterward it lurched from one crisis to another, constantly on the brink. However, that didn't stop the PhoeniX from wowing the crowds when it was unveiled, although it also left many feeling underwhelmed. At the time of writing, Saab's future was hanging in the balance; now the company might have a future thanks to the Chinese, but nothing is for certain in the automotive industry.

The idea of the PhoeniX was to show that Saab could survive, so the name was inspired; after all, this would be the symbol of a once-great car company rising from the ashes of the shell that was left when General Motors finally lost interest and disposed of the company in 2010.

When the PhoeniX was revealed, Saab Automobile's Executive Design Director Jason Castriota claimed: "Our company is being reborn and the PhoeniX is a celebration of the pioneering spirit and enthusiasm that took Saab into the automotive business. It ushers in a new generation of Saab design. We call it 'aeromotional,' adding passion and emotion to cool Scandinavian aesthetics."

Saab also reckoned that the PhoeniX would play a key role in its future models—but the company had no future. In the event, the 2011 Geneva Motor Show, held in the spring of that year, would be the last motor show in which Saab would take part.

Above: The PhoeniX was a great-looking car, but it was yet another case of too little, too late—and it wasn't enough to save the company, which went bust soon after.

Left to right: It's hard to find an angle that doesn't flatter the PhoeniX; the front end is especially neat, while the profile also looks purposeful.

Technology

Saab has a long history of using turbocharged gasoline engines and front-wheel drive—a combination that doesn't always mix successfully. With the PhoeniX, Saab didn't keep things that simple, because it had a hybrid power train with four-wheel drive.

Under that heavily sculpted hood and beneath its cargo deck, the PhoeniX propulsion system consisted of a highly efficient, 1.6-liter turbocharged gasoline engine driving the front wheels, which was combined with electric drive for the rear. The compact, all-aluminum engine produced 200 brake horsepower, while the electric motor was a 25-kilowatt (34-horsepower) unit powered by a small battery pack that was topped up by regenerative braking. This power train was no pie-in-the-sky concept either; Saab was developing it for its next generation of production cars, because it gave all the benefits of four-wheel drive but with reduced fuel consumption.

While the drivetrain was impressive, the PhoeniX's multimedia system was just as exciting. Dubbed iQon, it was based on Google's Android operating system. It included what Saab claimed were the best parts of cell phone technology and usability. The company was ambitious, too; users would be able to download a wide range of applications, online services, and multimedia functions provided through a Saab IQon store. More than 500 signals from different sensors in the vehicle measured, for example, vehicle speed, location and direction of travel, driver workload, yaw rate, steering wheel angle, engine speed and torque, inside and outside temperatures, barometric pressure, and the sun's position. And to think that at one time, a cutting-edge concept was one with a TV screen somewhere on the dash.

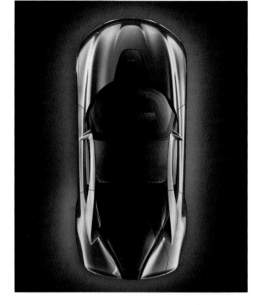

Top: The overhead view gives the best indication of all as to just how rounded the front end was; it looked sensational.

Middle: The dash was full of the latest tech, with an app-style display. One of the apps was this virtual analog clock.

Bottom: The small fenders that ran down each side of the car reduced lift and turbulence, as well as drag, so the Coefficient was just 0.25.

Design

With its roots in aeronautics, the "aeromotional" design for the PhoeniX was interesting, if a little contrived. It was this design language—a mixture of aeronautical and automotive with some emotion thrown in for good measure—that was intended to take center stage in Saab's forthcoming new models.

There's no doubt that the PhoeniX's bodywork was striking, but it's unlikely that it would have made you think of the rippling bodywork sheathed by the skinsuit of a speed skater. However, that's what Saab claimed it looked like.

The frontal styling featured a bold, stretched interpretation of Saab's signature three-port grille, the chromeless opening encompassing the full width of the front end. Saab's traditional central grille bar evolved into a body-colored fender form, with LED headlights and indicators fitted discreetly into the tips of the fender.

Below the grille, the main air intake area featured active shutters that closed at speed to improve aerodynamic efficiency while slim, body-colored small fenders carried the front foglights.

Flanking the roof were small fenders intended to resemble the vestigial wings of an aircraft. Shaped to collect turbulent air and direct it onto the Phoenix's rear deck, they increased high-speed stability by reducing rear lift; the result was a drag coefficient of just 0.25.

Inside the 2+2 cabin, simplicity and technology came to the forefront. A driver-focused instrument layout introduced the world to Saab's innovative IQon entertainment and communications system, with touch-screen functionality eliminating many of the more usual buttons and controls. The cabin embraced a minimalist feel, with slim competition-like seats and metalized interior sections—and it looked great with it.

At a Glance

Country of Manufacture
Sweden

Engine
Front-mounted, turbocharged four-cylinder with hybrid assistance

Displacement	1.6 liters
Power	200 bhp + 34 bhp
Torque	185 lb.-ft.

Drivetrain
Six-speed manual; four-wheel drive

Suspension, Wheels, and Brakes
Front suspension: MacPherson struts, aluminum lower A-arms, antiroll bar
Rear suspension: 5-link independent suspension, coil springs, shock absorbers, antiroll bar

Wheels: 20-in. (508-mm) alloys front and rear

Tires: 245/40 R20 front and rear

Front brakes: 15-in. (378-mm) ventilated discs with 6-piston calipers

Rear brakes: 13-in. (325-mm) ventilated discs with 4-piston calipers

Weights and Measurements

Wheelbase	101 in. (2,555 mm)
Length	173 in. (4,416 mm)
Width	74 in. (1,868 mm)
Height	52 in. (1,328 mm)
Drag coefficient	0.25

Performance

0–62 mph	5.9 seconds
Top speed	155 mph (250 km/h) (restricted)
CO_2 emissions	119 g/km
Debut:	Geneva 2011

SEAT Formula (1999)

At a time when many manufacturers were embarrassed into being more socially aware, SEAT bucked the trend at the 1999 Geneva Motor Show with the first showing of its Formula concept. It was unveiled as "bringing the excitement of competition driving to the highway, while not overlooking the comforts needed for more conventional driving."

The reality was that the Formula was just another two-seater sports car—although that didn't make it any less tempting a prospect. It was especially tempting because it was in the mold of the Lotus Elise and Vauxhall VX220, cars that put driving enjoyment and performance above all else. If it was comfort and equipment you were after, these were cars to be avoided, just like the Formula. However, if you wanted a white-knuckle ride every time you got behind the wheel—effectively a four-wheeled motorcycle experience—the Formula was the car for the job.

It was no coincidence that the Formula was so close in concept to the Lotus Elise, as Julian Thomson was an integral part of both projects, having joined the SEAT team as head of exterior design. He was the one who worked out how to package everything, but one thing he didn't do was introduce any form of weather protection. Utilizing an Elise-style tensioned fabric roof would have been easy enough, but with such a tight production schedule for the car's introduction, there simply wasn't time. In the end, the car wasn't produced, although it opened the world's eyes to the idea of SEAT being the sporty division of the VW/Audi Group. However, the company could have been so much sportier.

Above: You'd be hard pressed to call the Formula attractive, but it was certainly distinctive—especially with that color scheme.

Left to right: The proportions were pretty much spot on, thanks to the engine being mounted in the middle; it's a shame the car didn't make production.

Technology

SEAT didn't cut corners in trying to create a lightweight sports car that would be great fun to drive, so in a bid to reduce weight as far as possible, the chassis was built of aluminum. And rather than hide away such a beautifully crafted piece of engineering, it was proudly displayed within the cockpit.

The final weight was less than a ton (907 kilograms), and when this was combined with the 240 brake horsepower offered, there was never any doubt that performance would be electrifying—0 to 62 miles (100 kilometers) per hour was possible in just 4.8 seconds. Instrumentation was also kept to a minimum. To change gear, there was a conventionally located gear lever, or paddles on the steering wheel allowed ratios to be selected. Whichever option was chosen, it was all done electronically without the need for a clutch.

With SEAT part of the VW empire, it was only natural that the mechanicals would be familiar to countless numbers of VW, Audi, and Skoda drivers. To that end, the Formula used a 240–brake horsepower 2.0-liter turbocharged gasoline engine along with a six-speed sequential manual transmission. This power plant was a development of the excellent 1.8-liter unit, and in 2.0-liter form it was derived from the SEAT Cordoba World Rally Car. Front-wheel drive was also dispensed with, and with the rear wheels doing the driving, the Formula would have been every bit as much fun to drive as the looks promised.

Top: The Formula would have been a Lotus Elise rival if it had made production, because it was a lightweight, stripped-down sports car.

Middle: Instrumentation was kept to a minimum, with all the essential information displayed directly in front of the driver.

Bottom: The Elise theme continued inside, with the aluminum chassis on display throughout; there wasn't much luxury on show.

Design

As if the concept of a two-seater sports car wasn't eye-catching enough, SEAT also opted to paint the car fluorescent yellow to make sure it got noticed. Wheels of the largest possible diameter were the norm around this time—on road cars as well as concepts—so the Formula was equipped with 20-inch (508-millimeter) alloy ones.

The doors opened upward, being hinged at the front, and because of the aluminum body tub, there were huge sills that gave the car its strength and torsional stiffness. Such a construction meant the handling would be predictable, and with the adoption of active cooling and aerodynamic systems, there was little chance of reliability issues arising in everyday use.

Above 30 miles (50 kilometers) per hour the rear spoiler popped up to maintain downforce (and hence stability), while at the front there were adjustable cooling intakes that channeled just the right amount of air to the engine to make sure that it didn't overheat while also maintaining a high running temperature for maximum efficiency.

The cabin followed a minimalist approach; there was no point weighing the car down with unnecessary trim or equipment. However, despite this—and although the car's interior was exposed to the elements—it had climate control. In classic sports-car style, the instruments were presented in three separate pods, each one containing information on a pair of functions. The idea was that this would be as clear as possible, and in reality the analog/digital setup would prove very easy to read at a glance. Not that it would ultimately make any difference . . .

At a Glance

Country of Manufacture
Spain/Germany

Engine
Midmounted, turbocharged 20-valve gas, four cylinders

Displacement	2 liters
Power	240 bhp
Torque	217 lb.-ft.

Drivetrain
Six-speed sequential manual transmission, rear-wheel drive

Suspension, Wheels, and Brakes
Front suspension: Double wishbones with coil springs

Rear suspension: Double wishbones with coil springs

Front wheels/tires: 7.5x20 with 205/45 R20 tires

Rear wheels/tires: 9x20 with 255/35 R20 tires

Weights and Measurements

Curb weight	1,984 lb. (900 kg)
Wheelbase	99 in. (2,523 mm)
Length	155 in. (3,943 mm)
Width	69 in. (1,758 mm)
Height	45 in. (1,152 mm)

Performance

0–62 mph	4.8 seconds
Top speed	147 mph (237 km/h)

Debut:	Geneva 1999
Design director:	Julian Thomson

Smart ForSpeed (2011)

When Mercedes set up its Smart division in the late 1990s, little did it know the trouble that was ahead. Indeed, the Smart was never intended to be a Mercedes project; it was originally set up by Volkswagen with Swatch entrepreneur Nicholas Hayek. When Volkswagen bailed out in 1993, Mercedes reckoned this diminutive city car project was too good an opportunity to miss. By the time the first cars hit the market in 1998, their production was being bankrolled almost entirely by Mercedes; Hayek would bail out completely within months.

Wonderfully designed and engineered, the Smart Coupé was fundamentally flawed in that it was too costly to compete with conventional four-seater cars that were more practical and affordable. That didn't stop Smart from pressing on with the development of a bigger version, the ForFour, along with a little mid-engine sports car, the Coupé and Roadster; by this time, the classic two seater had been renamed the ForTwo. These extra elements of the Smart brand would be short-lived; they were costly to make, costly to buy, and their appeal proved very limited. That left Smart to continue only with its ForTwo. Along the way there was also the wild—and stupidly expensive—limited-run Crossblade, which would prove to be the forerunner of the ForSpeed concept of 2011.

With no windshield—or indeed any protection from the elements at all—the Crossblade was one of those cars that just made no sense, yet Smart still managed to sell a few of them. It was always meant to be made in only tiny numbers, but its lack of usability and a sky-high price meant it was even more exclusive than Smart had first anticipated.

None of this stopped Smart from developing a concept for the 2011 Geneva Motor Show that was effectively an update of this earlier wacky design. Fully driveable and generally applauded by the motoring press, there was clearly an opportunity for something like the ForSpeed to enter limited production. Whether or not Smart could make such a car at a price that was remotely palatable, however, was altogether a different matter.

Above: When the ForSpeed was being first designed, its eco worthiness was highlighted by green bands on the tires.

Left to right: By the time the ForSpeed was a real car, the green tires had gone, but the car lost none of its visual impact in the translation from the drawing board.

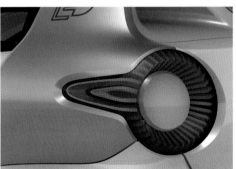

Technology

The key technology showcased by the ForSpeed was its electric drive propulsion system, as already seen in Smart's production ForTwo. Crucially, because all electric cars were costly, the ForSpeed wouldn't be that much more expensive than its rivals—but the chances would be that any rival would be a lot more usable.

At the heart of the ForSpeed was a 30-kilowatt magneto-electric motor, which was installed at the rear. Pressing a button in the center console activated a boost function that provided an extra 5 kilowatts for a short time, so the car could overtake with greater haste. Without using this extra surge of power, the ForTwo could accelerate from a standing start to 40 miles (64 kilometers) per hour in just 5.5 seconds, before running out of puff at 80 miles (129 kilometers) per hour.

Crucially, at this point in Smart's development, it had already been selling electric cars around the globe and had received a lot of feedback from its customers about what the cars were like to live with in the real world. Smart claimed that as a result, it had engineered the ForTwo to provide a level of performance and usability with which real-world customers could live.

Power came from a lithium-ion battery capable of storing up to 16.5 kilowatt hours of electrical energy; it could be charged via a conventional 220-volt outlet and would provide up to 85 miles (137 kilometers) of travel on a single charge. For those in a hurry, there was also a quick-charging facility, which would charge the batteries to a level of 80 percent in 45 minutes.

In a bid to make the ForSpeed as efficient as possible, the aeroscreen incorporated photovoltaic cells that fed solar power to the onboard electrical system. It wouldn't have boosted the batteries by much, but every little bit helps.

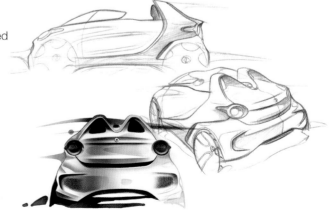

Opposite, top: To drain the batteries as slowly as possible, there were ultra-efficient LED lights fitted front and rear.

Opposite, middle: Smart has always produced rounded cars, but the ForSpeed was the most curvacious yet; there wasn't a straight edge in sight.

Opposite, bottom: These sketches show the influence of the Smart Crossblade, a production car sold around a decade earlier.

Above: The ForSpeed's rear end was both solidly wide and sporty, reminiscent of the Mini.

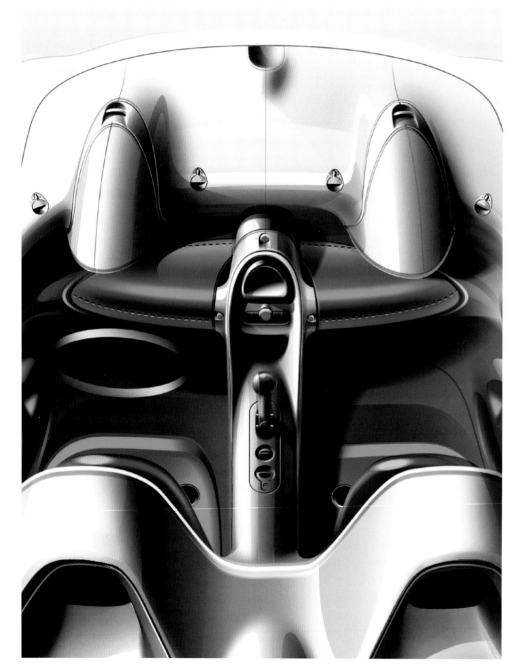

Left: You wouldn't expect a bland interior with exterior lines like the ForSpeed's—and you didn't get one, but it was tasteful.

Right, above: Those LED lights weren't just efficient; they were also very compact and capable of being molded to pretty much any shape.

Right, below: Smart has always focused on two-tone color themes to distinguish its cars; this proposal worked especially well.

Design

When the ForSpeed was unveiled, Smart claimed that it "combines responsibility and emotional appeal in a new and pleasurable way." Try telling that to a hapless owner stuck by the side of the road in the middle of nowhere, with the rain lashing down because the battery has gone dead. Well maybe that's a bit unfair, and it's definitely cynical, but it was hard to see the ForSpeed selling in anything other than tiny numbers if it had made it to market.

However, while it may have been impractical, there was no denying that the ForSpeed featured some superb design elements. There was no roof, no windows, and nothing more than an aeroscreen to keep the bugs out of its occupants' teeth, but here was a car that looked as though it had come from the design studios of Apple, such was its modernity.

There was gloss white plastic everywhere, along with striking lighting that featured LEDs throughout. The cabin was swathed in gloss white, too, accentuated by green elements such as the four-point seat belts and the shelf under the cockpit that provided much-needed stowage space. The control elements used most frequently were finished in brown leather, while the load-bearing structural components featured a matte silver finish. So, while it didn't really stand much chance of ever seeing the light of day as a production car, the ForSpeed sure looked good inside and out.

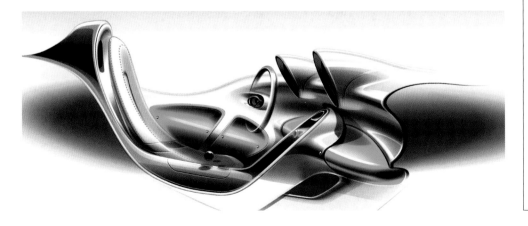

At a Glance

Country of Manufacture
Germany

Engine
Rear-mounted 30-kW electric motor powered by a 16.5-kWh lithium-ion battery

Power | 30 kW with 5 Kw overboost facility

Drivetrain
Rear-wheel drive

Suspension, Wheels, and Brakes
Front tires: 205/35 R18

Rear tires: 235/30 R18

Weights and Measurements
Wheelbase	74 in. (1,870 mm)
Length	106 in. (2,700 mm)
Width	61 in. (1,560 mm)

Performance
0–62 mph	5.5 seconds
Top speed	75 mph (121 km/h)
Range	85 miles (137 km)
Debut:	Geneva 2011

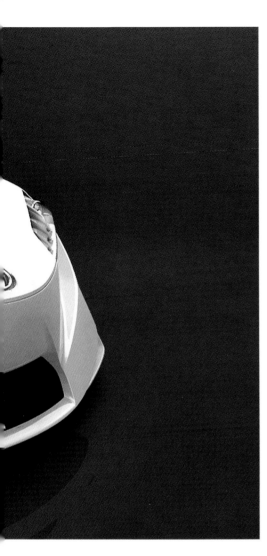

Toyota FT-HS (2007)

At the 2007 Geneva Motor Show, Toyota unveiled its new Auris: a car that the company claimed was "a landmark in the European C segment." Alongside this was the FT-HS (Future Toyota Hybrid Sports) concept—a vision of the future that was genuinely exciting. If ever you needed an example of how far removed from reality a decent concept is, here was a perfect one. Dull, derivative small hatch meets excitingly styled technology-laden car of the future—it's not hard to decide which one makes more of a mark on the automotive landscape.

For a company renowned for producing one unremarkable design after another, Toyota had a curious knack of producing great-looking concepts. However, frustratingly, the eye-catching designs of these studies never seemed to translate into the company's production offerings. The FT-HS was one of a series of eye-catching Toyota concepts of the period, and it was particularly interesting because it was aimed at a segment that this Japanese company had abandoned when it gave up on its Celica coupé.

Toyota had been the market leader in hybrid technology ever since its Prius had arrived in 1998. In some markets, many Lexus models were sold in only hybrid form, so it came as no surprise that this particular concept featured a gasoline/electric drivetrain. Until this point, nobody had offered an electric sports car; such technology was seen really as the domain of more practical family cars. However, before long the Tesla supercar would go on sale, and while weight, top speed, and range would continue to be limiting factors with electric cars, the available acceleration was often one of the most appealing facets.

Crucially, Toyota revealed that the FT-HS was part of its commitment to develop a full and wide range of hybrid cars, proving that it didn't see the future of hybrid technology as lying solely with dull family transport.

Above: The name may have been terminally bland, but the looks of the FT-HS were anything but; this was one mean-looking car.

Left to right: The FT-HS was meant to jump-start Toyota's design studios into producing more desirable-looking production models.

Technology

The premise of the FT-HS was to create a sustainable sports car for the twenty-first century. In other words, Toyota's aim was to come up with the most efficient sports car possible, without diluting the driving experience. That might sound like a tall order, but one of the benefits of the gasoline/electric drivetrain is that there's a much larger amount of torque availabe than in a conventionally driven car. And with more torque, meaning more acceleration, it makes for a pretty good starting point.

The good news continued with the FT-HS's configuration; up front there was a free-revving 3.5-liter V6 engine, which drove the rear wheels. So while a mid-engine setup may have offered a purer driving experience, at least the power went to the right end of the car. With around 400 brake horsepower on tap, there was plenty of power, too.

Based on an all-new platform, there were MacPherson struts, coil springs, and antiroll bars front and rear, so the drivetrain didn't really feature much in the way of cutting-edge technology. However, inside it was a different matter. All of the car's important functions and details were presented almost exclusively to the driver. For example, touch-trace sensors surrounded the driver and acted as tactile guides for finger controls when traveling at high speeds. To top things off, a telescoping hubless steering wheel incorporated semiautomatic paddle shifters—the sure sign of a driver's car.

Top: While the exterior looked futuristic, the interior was much more so; things kicked off with the use of a single-spoke steering wheel.

Middle: Four exhaust pipes suggest a hefty V8 being fitted, but there was actually a V6, boosted by an electric hybrid power train.

Bottom: The FT-HS was bristling with gorgeous details, such as LED lighting, scoops, and spoilers all over the place.

Design

For some reason, Japanese carmakers just love to overcomplicate things, so instead of talking about the design features of the FT-HS, Toyota insisted on muddying the waters by introducing not one but two design languages: J-Factor and Vibrant Clarity. The first provided a form with global visual appeal, while the second was a "combination of perfect imbalance, freeform geometrics, and integrated component architecture." Um, right.

What all this boiled down to was a sleek four-seat coupé that looked superb and featured a cool retractable roof. Except there was a snag: The roof retracted into the space usually allocated to the rear seats, so you could either carry four people or enjoy some wind in your hair—but not both.

A product of Toyota California-based CALTY design studio, this car was a mass of scoops, slats, and spoilers, with the FT-HS looking aggressive from all angles. It was also surprisingly efficient aerodynamically; many of the exterior details were included to smooth airflow while also adding downforce.

Many of the features were aerospace-inspired, such as the LED lighting, although by this point such technology had already started to appear in mainstream production cars. This aeronautical theme continued inside as well, with a steering wheel and dash that looked more like something from a jet fighter; the use of carbon fiber and titanium throughout only helped to reinforce this feel.

At a Glance

Country of Manufacture
Japan/USA

Engine
Front-mounted, normally aspirated gas V6 with electric assistance

Displacement	3.5 liters
Power	400 bhp approx.

Drivetrain
Semiautomatic transmission, rear-wheel drive

Suspension, Wheels, and Brakes
Front suspension: MacPherson struts, coil springs, and antiroll bar

Rear suspension: MacPherson struts, coil springs, and antiroll bar

Carbon-fiber wheels, 21 in. (533 mm) in diameter

Front tires: 245/35 R21

Rear tires: 285/30 R21

Weights and Measurements

Wheelbase	104 in. (2,650 mm)
Length	170 in. (4,325 mm)
Width	73 in. (1,860 mm)
Height	51 in. (1,290 mm)

Performance

0–62 mph	4 seconds approx.

Debut:	Detroit 2007
Exterior designer:	Alex Shen

Volkswagen XL1 (2011)

If you were asked to name the most conservative carmakers in the world, the chances are that Volkswagen would be in there somewhere. After all, with its cars all looking basically the same, and each one representing little more than an evolution of the previous model, it's not hard to spot a Volkswagen at a glance.

However, under the skin the company's cars have frequently been much more innovative than you might expect. And although the XL1 was far from a production reality, nowhere was Volkswagen's creativity more evident than with this ultraefficient city car.

From the outset, the premise of the XL1 was to produce the world's most efficient car—and this was no theoretical design study, because it had to be fully operational. As a result, the XL1 was built of lightweight materials and was incredibly efficient aerodynamically, while power came from an advanced diesel/electric hybrid power train.

The XL1 was the follow up to the 1-liter of 2002, another ultraslippery two seater that sipped diesel at the incredibly parsimonious rate of just 1 liter for every 100 kilometers—equivalent to 283 miles per gallon. The XL1 took that impressive figure and improved on it by around ten percent, which meant that on the official test cycle it could achieve an extremely impressive 313 miles per gallon. Keeping in mind that real-world fuel economy is often around 20 percent worse than the official figures, this would still put the XL1's fuel consumption at 250 miles per gallon—which would be at least three times more efficient than the most frugal production cars of the time.

However, those production cars would have been less compromised than the XL1, which had pretty much no luggage carrying capacity. Despite such impracticality, Volkswagen talked seriously about putting the car into limited production. It hasn't happened yet, and if it does, the asking price will likely be astronomical—but just think of the fuel savings.

Above: The XL1 was an incredible feat of engineering, because it was capable of transporting two people, yet it could manage more than 300 mpg.

Left to right: The key to the XL's amazing efficiency was its ultralightweight construction paired with an incredibly slippery shape.

Technology

It would have been easy for Volkswagen to simply fit an electric motor to the XL1 and say it emitted no CO_2 while enjoying usable performance and an ample range. However, the company was much more clever than that; instead, it installed a tiny diesel engine that was optimized for efficiency, while also fitting a hybrid power train that could capture the energy otherwise lost through braking—a regenerative braking system.

That engine was a two-cylinder turbodiesel unit that displaced just 48.8 ci (800 cc), tuned to give 47 brake horsepower and 88 lb.-ft. of torque. On its own, this would have given perfectly decent performance around town, but with the hybrid drivetrain assisting, there was a total of 74 brake horsepower and 162 lb.-ft. of torque available, which made things surprisingly sprightly for such a frugal machine.

That hybrid drivetrain consisted of a 20-kilowatt motor powered by a lithium-ion battery; power was transmitted to the rear wheels via a seven-speed dual-clutch semiautomatic transmission. There was the option of a fully automatic mode but without the usual power loss penalties of a torque-converter automatic transmission.

Importantly, while the battery pack could be topped up through regenerative braking or by the diesel engine, it could also be recharged from a conventional domestic power outlet. As a result, through the use of renewable energies, the XL1's envionmental impact could be minimized.

Top: The XL1 may have been one of the most advanced cars ever made, but that didn't stop Volkswagen from fitting a low-key interior.

Middle: With parts carried over from Volkswagen's regular production cars, the cabin was beautifully made but visually unexciting.

Bottom: Lightweight materials were used throughout the XL's construction, most notably aluminum for the main structure.

Opposite: The XLI featured a supercar-esque beetle-wing door design.

Design

The most striking thing about the XL1 was its incredibly aerodynamic fighter jet–style silhouette. With the top of its canopy just 46 inches (1,156 millimeters) off the ground—a contemporary Polo was 58 inches (1,462 millimeters) tall—the XL1 was astonishingly low slung. This helped to reduce wind resistance, while the XL1's weight was cut dramatically thanks to the use of a carbon fiber unibody.

The XL1 was widest at the front; from there it tapered, so that in profile its shape represented that of a dolphin. Meanwhile, in profile the roofline represented a continuous arc from the A-pillar right to the back, while the rear wheels were fully covered to cut drag even more. Predictably, there were no door-mounted mirrors, because they'd have affected the aerodynamics; instead, there were small cameras to relay images to screens inside the cockpit.

One of the most interesting details of the XL's design was the doors, which were more like the kind of thing you'd expect on a supercar. Hinged at the base of the A-pillars and just above the windshield, this beetle-wing design gave the XL1 an exotic air, even if its performance was far from exotic.

At a Glance

Country of Manufacture
Germany

Engine
Rear-mounted, turbodiesel two-cylinder with electric motor assistance via a lithium-ion battery

Displacement	49 ci (800 cc)
Power	47 bhp (+27 bhp from the motor)
Torque	88 lb.-ft. (+74 lb.-ft. from the motor)

Drivetrain
Seven-speed semiautomatic transmission, rear-wheel drive

Suspension, Wheels, and Brakes
Unavailable

Weights and Measurements

Curb weight	1,753 lb. (795 kg)
Wheelbase	88 in. (2,224 mm)
Length	153 in. (3,888 mm)
Width	66 in. (1,665 mm)
Height	46 in. (1,156 mm)

Performance

0–62 mph	11.9 seconds
Top speed	100 mph (160 km) (limited)
Fuel consumption	313 mpg
CO_2 emissions	24 g/km
Range (electric only)	22 miles (35 km)
Range (electric/TDI)	344 miles (553 km)
Drag coefficient	0.186
Debut:	Qatar 2011

Volvo YCC (2004)

It's interesting that although Volvo was behind one of the very first concept cars, as already revealed in the introduction to this book, it's a company that until the 1980s focused almost exclusively on creating production cars. Even when Volvo did build a concept in the 1980s or beyond, it was generally an early view of a production model or it was a test bed for safety technologies, such as a new restraint system or a new type of crash structure.

For example, the ECC of 1992 was effectively an early view of the original S60 and S80, while the VCC was a preview of the 700 Series that would appear in 1982. Indeed, take a look at just about any concept to come from Volvo and it's been followed at some stage by a production model that looks largely similar. However, there has been a notable exception to this rule and that's the YCC, or the awkwardly named Your Concept Car. The idea behind the car cropped up in 2001, when Marti Barletta paid a visit to Volvo. An American expert on female consumer patterns, Barletta suggested that Volvo put together an all-female team to come up with a car that would meet the needs and expectations of women; intriguingly, her argument went that if they could do this, any male potential customers would be happy, because they're far less demanding than their female counterparts.

By the summer of 2002, the all-women team had been assembled; their task was to create the perfect car for the modern, independent professional woman. By this stage, more than half of Volvo's U.S. buyers were women, and Volvo's research suggested that women buyers in the premium segment were the most demanding consumers of all; if the company could keep them happy, it could keep anyone happy!

Above: Most of Volvo's concept cars have given a glimpse of a future production model, but not here; it's never built a coupé like this.

Left to right: It's a shame the YCC never made production; it looked sleek and sporty, and those gull-wing doors worked wonderfully.

Technology

Long before it became fashionable, Volvo adopted a green ethic. As a result, its cars were among the greenest available, although they had a reputation for being gas guzzlers. When it came to working out what mechanicals to fit to the YCC, it wasn't a difficult choice to make; it would have the five-cylinder PZEV (partial zero emissions vehicle) gasoline unit that was already capable of meeting the world's most stringent emissions regulations: those of California.

Capable of generating a handy 215 brake horsepower, this 2.5-liter unit featured what was then termed ISG, or integrated starter-generator; since then, the technology has generally become known as stop/start or intelligent stop and go (so still ISG). The idea of the technology was that it would switch the engine off when the car came to a halt, and when the accelerator was pressed, it would automatically set the engine running again.

The engine drove the front wheels via a six-speed semiautomatic transmission, which meant that the driver could choose the gears manually or could leave the car to do everything—the idea being that in the latter mode the car would be even more frugal thanks to its computer selecting the optimum change-up or change-down points. Those gears were selected through using paddle shifts on either side of the steering wheel—a feature that would become increasingly popular in time, but which was still rare when the YCC was unveiled.

Also, in a bid to cut fuel consumption at speed, there was a height-adjustable suspension system fitted. The car would lower itself automatically when traveling quickly, but when driving more slowly the car's ride height could be raised to negotiate speed bumps or other hazards.

Top: With its shallow glasshouse and thick pillars, the cabin could easily feel cramped, which is why light colors were used throughout.

Middle: With patterns and colors like that, it was clear that no men were allowed to be part of the cabin design process.

Bottom: In a bid to make the YCC as easy to drive as possible, there was a semiautomatic transmission fitted, with a sequential manual mode.

Design

Of course, an excellent design inside and out was essential for the YCC, but as you'd expect, the designers' brief was much wider than that. Particular attention had to be paid to things, such as storage, usability, and access. Easy parking, personalization opportunities, and good visibility were important, too.

Taking all these things into account, it was reckoned that gull-wing doors would provide the best method of getting in and out. Naturally, there was power assistance, but in an especially innovative twist the car would detect when you'd moved alongside it and the door would automatically open for you. So if you had your hands full, you wouldn't have to put everything down and then wrestle with the mechanism.

Ease of parking was taken into account with a park-assist program that would self-park the car, thanks to a series of sensors. However, it was visibility that was at the forefront of much of the interior and exterior design; the driving position and line of vision are crucial for safety and comfort. So when ordering your YCC, your whole body would be scanned at the dealership, and then the data on your relative proportions (height, leg length, arm length) would be used to define a driving position just for you.

This information would be stored in digital form on your personal key, and once you climbed into the driver's seat and docked your key in the center console, the seat, steering wheel, pedals, head restraint, and seat belt would all be adjusted automatically.

The full side view of the YCC: small and perfectly formed.

At a Glance

Country of Manufacture
Sweden

Engine
Front-mounted, normally aspirated five-cylinder gas with stop and start

Displacement	154 ci (2,521 cc)
Power	215 bhp

Drivetrain
Six-speed semiautomatic transmission, front-wheel drive

Debut:	Geneva 2004
Design director:	Maria Widell Christiansen
Exterior designer:	Anna Rosén
Interior designer:	Cynthia Charwick

Index

1, 2, 3 . . .

A

B

C

D

E

F

G

H

I

J

L